What Africans Stand to Lose

Underscores Trump's *shithole* slur, and actions that reinforce hurting stereotypes!

WILLIAMS EKANEM

THE
CORNERSTONE
P U B L I S H I N G

What Africans Stand to Lose

Underscores Trump's *shithole* slur, and actions that reinforce hurting stereotypes!

Cornerstone Publishing
A Division of Cornerstone Creativity Group LLC
Phone: +1(516) 547-4999
info@thecornerstonepublishers.com
www.thecornerstonepublishers.com

To order bulk copies of this book or to contact the author please email: ekanwills@gmail.com

This book is dedicated to all black Africans

who migrate to the United States,

roll up their sleeves

and work hard to raise their heads above water.

Contents

Thinking Out Loud

There seems to be no end in sight to President Donald Trump's uncouth mannerism and leadership, because he may just be texting or saying the next outlandish thing, as you read this book.

Presidential historians, ethics custodians, concerned individuals have since lost count of the bizarre actions and statements from this president. Although we have now inadvertently gotten used to Trump's insults on people, institutions, nations and common sense, they must nonetheless be documented, not necessarily for today, but for tomorrow; for the next generation and for posterity. This is the primary reason for this book.

No individual, group, profession, institution or country is spared from Trump's daily insults - not even the Pope or the dead. Trump has told his intelligence chiefs to 'go back to school.' One way or the other, everyone else, except members of his family and of course his mentor, Vladimir Putin, has been hit with his verbal attacks, often characterized by conspiracy theories, blatant lies and, for the nonwhites, racial undertones.

My country, the United States of America, before Trump's presidency, used to be the world's beacon of hope and moral ethics, but that has since changed. It is now being laughed at by other foreign leaders. It had never been this bad, and it's getting worse by the day, unfortunately.

The dreadful truth is that this President has created an alternate universe for himself, where his small circle of loyalists live to revere him. They fawn all over him as the best thing ever, and as Trump himself would say in his characteristic hyperbole, it is "like the world has never seen." The situation is not only unfortunate, but pathetic.

Discerning Americans and the world at large are getting used to Trump's divide and rule politics, but what is getting rather difficult to comprehend is his penchant for inciting cynicism within and between diverse groups, races and cultures. Little wonder an ex-White House staff turned author described staffers at the White House as, a "team of vipers."

To our very face, Trump called Mexicans rapists and said that a federal judge could not be fair to him because he was Hispanic. Trump reportedly wondered, "Why do we need more Haitians?" urging, "Take them out." He said, "Nigerians live in huts" and that he did not want "a single dollar" go to ravaged Puerto Rico, a US territory. And the list goes on. That is supposed to be the President of the free world talking! Unbelievable.

Right thinking members of the public are flabbergasted at the vituperation from a sitting President, not of a third world country, but of the United States of America, the world's leading country. Kurt Bardella wrote in HuffPost recently that "Trump has shown himself to be a small man willing to degrade and insult people with disabilities, people of color, immigrants, veterans, the dead, sexual assault survivors, women, etc."

Bardella, a former spokesman for the House Oversight and Government Reform Committee, who had left the Republican Party to join Democratic Party aptly added that, "he has no shortage of vulnerabilities ripe for attack."

Masha Gessen of the New Yorker describes Trump's often vulgar comments as "degradation of the public sphere."

One can go on and on and can say without any contradiction that dishing out invective is Trump's modus operandi. It was apparently the reason he couldn't hold back, during an immigration meeting at the White House, from referring to immigrants from sub-Saharan Africa as people from *"shithole"* countries; or referring to Vice President, Joe Biden, even during his compulsive daily coronavirus briefing, as "Sleepy Joe", not minding the fact that people are dying in large numbers on a daily basis.

This book takes that slur on black Africans very seriously. The author attempts to recount that unfortunate occurrence from a reporter's perspective, and then digs deep to see how other United States Presidents engaged with people in sub-Saharan Africa.

The book then revisits the rather murky issue of aid to Africa. In mimicking Trump, the writer enumerates what sub-Saharan Africans stand to lose or are already losing from his contemptuous presidential style.

The writer, in the closing chapters, attempts to debunk various stereotypes attached to people from that part of the world and ends with showcasing the vast potentials of these countries and their people.

CHAPTER ONE

Trump's Backhanded Compliments to Black Africans

I don't know about you, but from the weird nature of the election that brought Donald Trump to office as United States President, I am sure many people did not know what to expect. This was even more so in the immigrant community, and especially with the people and nations from sub-Saharan Africa.

Going by Trump's continuous vilification of nonwhites - from the day he announced his intention to run for the office of the President of the United States, and on winning the election - the early days of his presidency became a nervous moment for most immigrants. The anxiety was heightened by the travel ban and its attendant crisis, just after inauguration.

However, for those in sub-Saharan Africa, the

waiting game to know what to expect did not last too long, as the new United States President gave an inkling of the direction of his administration towards the region during his first meeting of the United Nations General Assembly in 2017.

At the sidelines of the UN gathering, the then newly elected President Trump hosted a maiden lunch meeting with African leaders from Cote d'Ivoire, Ethiopia, Ghana, Namibia, Nigeria, Senegal, South Africa and Uganda. Media reports of the meeting have it that Trump told the African leaders that Africa has tremendous business potentials, adding, "I have so many friends going to your countries, trying to get rich. I congratulate you, they're spending a lot of money. It's really become a place they have to go, that they want to go."

It is hard to say if that statement was Trump's frank assessment of the region (that would be absurd, going by the myriad of challenges of the region) or an innuendo to send a message to the African leaders. Whatever it was, the message was clear enough to reveal the direction of the President's Africa policy, whenever it would be rolled out. With Trump's perception of the region as a destination for those "trying to get rich", anyone should know that there would not be much, if any, to cheer from the new US President in terms of help or assistance to the region.

If nothing else, such a statement signaled that the days of help to the region may be over; and gone are the days that the USA gives funding to needy African countries for developmental assistance. That indication from the new US President might not have been a good omen for African leaders, some of whom imprudently depend almost entirely on foreign aid.

With his resolute "America First" policy, President Trump said it loud and clear, that the days of big brother USA have run out, because, in his reasoning, American citizens also need the money. To Trump, such charity now begins and probably stops at home, a position that draws many people to him and his administration.

Covert Disclosure

It can as well be said that Trump used the opportunity of his maiden meeting with the African leaders to advertently make his mindset on Africa known, while also giving an insight into his policy direction in future US-Africa relations during his administration.

But suffice it to say that a lot of literary conjectures followed the rather frank remark by President Trump, after that meeting. This writer also wrote an article then that was published in various pan-

African publications, one of which was *Next Money*. The article is reproduced below:

Deconstructing Trump's Innuendo to African Leaders

African leaders do not need to wait any longer for the direction of the Trump administration's Africa policy, if it ever comes, because there would not be much to cheer about. Going by the well-publicized statement the United States President made to a group of African heads of state on September 20, at the sidelines of the 72nd session of the United Nations General Assembly in New York, the days of aids windfall are over.

Gone are the days that through its various agencies like USAID, the USA doles out large chunk of funds to needy African countries to assist in one developmental goal or the other, to the delight of the leaders, with some of them shamelessly misappropriating the funds without conscience.

With his resolute "America First," policy, President Trump says it loudly that the days of big brother USA have run out, because, in his reasoning, American citizens also need the money. To Trump, such charity now begins and stops at home.

While hosting a luncheon for leaders of Cote d'Ivoire, Ethiopia, Ghana, Guinea, Namibia, Nigeria, Senegal, South Africa and Uganda during the UN General

Assembly, Trump laid bare his mind on Africa, which gives insight into whatever policy content in future US-Africa relations.

"Africa has tremendous business potential. I have so many friends going to your countries trying to get rich. I congratulate you. They're spending a lot of money. It's really become a place they have to go, that they want to go," Trump was reported to have said during the parley.

In deconstructing Trump's perception of Sub-Saharan Africa (SSA) through the above statement, first, it can be argued that from his transactional approach to everything, the US President preempted the African leaders in their usual sing song of poverty in the continent. Don't even talk about being poor because, "I have so many friends going to your countries trying to get rich," Trump seemed to be telling them indirectly. As a self-proclaimed world-class negotiator, Trump quickly arrived at where the African leaders may have planned to go at the meeting, thus stopping them from repeating the rather trite excuse of lack of financial resources.

Secondly, the African leaders may have planned to use the opportunity of a face-to-face meeting with the new US President to push their other card—ecological and socio-political issues like crime and conflicts as reasons to deserve assistance. Again, Trump shot them down already by telling them straight to their face that, "Africa has tremendous potentials." Trump sure has a point here, because Africa is home to 1.2 billion people in 54 countries and is by any reckoning not short of human and material resources, rather what the continent is short of are leaders with sincere and good managers of resources.

According to the World Bank, "six of the world's ten fastest growing economies are in Africa." In its Economic Outlook (June 2017) for instance, the World Bank stated that Growth in "SSA is forecast to pick up to 2.6 percent in 2017, and average 3.4 percent in 2018-19, slightly above population growth. The recovery is predicated on moderately rising commodity prices and reforms to tackle macroeconomic imbalances."

Thirdly, although most African leaders may reluctantly agree that their countries have tremendous potentials, but they would quickly point at the prevalent low purchasing power that has inhibited the citizenry from maximizing such potentials. But the US President undercut that argument by telling them that, "they are spending a lot of money."

In agreeing with Trump, most African leaders and the elite do actually spend a lot of money, most times on the wrong things, and at tax payers' expense like marrying more wives, assembling fleet of cars, buying properties abroad, extravagant shopping spree abroad by wives/concubines, and even stashing considerable amounts in foreign bank accounts.

Most African leaders do not have good history in managing government funds. There usually is a very thin line, if any, between public funds and personal income, a reason majority of the countries in SSA sit tight in the lowest rung of the transparency index.

According to Jose Ugaz, Chair of Transparency International in the 2016 report, " in too many countries, people are deprived of their most basic needs and go to bed hungry every night because of corruption, while the powerful and corrupt enjoy lavish lifestyles with impunity."

Lastly, Trump also disabused whatever notion the African leaders would want to present to him as a case for more aids due to brain drain, where professionals from various walks of life are leaving the continent in droves for greener pastures abroad, especially USA. Instead of buying the argument, the US President informed the leaders that their countries have, " really become a place his friends have to go, they want to go, and get rich."

The entire statement qualifies for the dictionary meaning of an innuendo, an indirect or subtle reference to the true state of affairs in most African countries, which the leaders may not want to admit.

As it is now, Trump has pulled the rug from under their feet as the largesse would not be coming in as usual. It is therefore a time for African leaders to be more discerning to their environment. With more determination, honesty and creativity, they can indeed make their various countries where people would really want to go.

This has become even more expedient going by Trump's apparent lack of enthusiasm for Africa, which was first on display at the Group of 20 summit in Hamburg, Germany in July when he had to vacate his sit for Ivanka, his daughter, when it was time for talks on African development.

This was also manifested during his address to the general assembly with just a sentence towards the end of his speech praising the African Union and UN led peacekeeping missions and a second praise for America in leading humanitarian assistance and relief efforts in South Sudan, Somalia and Northern Nigeria.

That Africa is not a front-burner concern for the Trump administration can further be seen in lack of not only an African policy, almost a year since its inception, but also endorsement of minimal engagement by abolishing office of special envoy to Sudan and South Sudan by Rex Tillerson, Secretary of State in August to save $5 million.

The crippling cuts to Africa was brought to head in the 2018 budget proposals that cut aid from $8 billion to $5.2 billion, with new emphasis only on security and military.

These cuts, according to the UN, are already having real-live consequences with millions of people on the brink of starvation in South-Sudan, Somalia and Nigeria and may be counterproductive, even to the USA.

This is because, as reflected by Uju Okoye, a Toronto-based researcher on African politics, "where there is hunger, there is anger and conflict; therefore, Trump's aim of cutting cost at any cost leaves Africa's myriad hotspots even more vulnerable and inimical to world peace."

CHAPTER TWO

Again, Caught in a Web of Lies!

More than three years into his presidency, Trump has not traveled to any African country. The most he has met with African leaders is at world meetings. It does not appear that whatever interaction Trump has had with African leaders at the sidelines of the United Nations General Assembly meetings has in any way changed his preconceived notion of the people of sub-Saharan Africa, more generally known as black Africa.

On January 11, 2018, during an immigration meeting at the White House, the US President was widely reported to have used vulgar language to describe black Africans as people from "*shithole*" countries. That President Trump constantly peddles mistruths is common knowledge, and in this instance, he tried it again nevertheless. He characteristically sent out a tweet to deny using such uncouth language on an entire continent, and by extension, an entire race. Below is the tweet:

"The language used by me at the DACA meeting was tough, but this was not the language used." "What was really tough was the outlandish proposal made – a big setback for DACA!" — Donald J. Trump (@realDonaldTrump) <u>January 12, 2018</u>

Notwithstanding the tweet, those at the meeting who do not owe Trump any apology spoke out on what actually transpired at the White House bipartisan meeting on immigration reforms, which unfortunately ended in a fiasco. Democratic Senator, Dick Durbin, representing Illinois, who was one of those at the meeting, was widely reported after the meeting to have stated that President Trump repeatedly described African nations as *"shithole"* countries.

The Illinois Senator told reporters that Trump's tweet denying using the term is "not true, disclosing that Trump said "hate-filled things" and "he said them repeatedly."

Failed Whitewashing

Now caught in the web of lies about his slur on black Africans and the attendant negative effect on him and his administration, aides of the President struggled hard to deny that the vulgar language on black African countries ever happened. However, the denial was difficult to establish, because the rebuttal from those at the meeting was so strong and emphatic; not even those from the President's party at the meeting could offer a convincing counter explanation. The situation became so messy that administration officials backed down from further attempts to deny the slur.

Instant denunciations of the statement from both within and outside the United States and the African continent were extraordinary. The backlash was fierce because nobody had ever seen or heard of such vulgarity from any country's leader, let alone the President of the United States, not even at war times.

The African Union (AU), a new name for the erstwhile Organization of African Unity (OAU) told the Associated Press, then, that it was "alarmed," by Trump's comments. Speaking on behalf of the continental body, the African Union spokesperson, Ebba Kalondo said, "Given the historical reality of how many Africans arrived in the United States as slaves, this statement flies in the face of all accepted behavior and practice."

It must be mentioned that some African leaders found themselves in an awkward position, condemning the statement. As top recipients of US aid, some leaders, according to reports, hesitated to jeopardize their relationship with the United States by criticizing Trump; but others did not hide their disdain for the withering remark.

Among the latter group was Botswana government that described Trump's statement as "reprehensible and racist". Uganda's State Minister for International Relations, Henry Oryem, described the vulgar statement as "unfortunate and regrettable," coming from an American leader.

Ghana's President, Nana Akufo-Addo, tweeted, "We are certainly not a *shithole* country."

President Macky Sall of Senegal in a statement said he was shocked and that "Africa and the black race merit the respect and consideration of all." The African National Congress, the ruling party in South Africa, called it "extremely offensive".

The wave of global outrage to the profanity grew, with the chairman of the Congressional Black Caucus in the US Congress, Representative Cedric Richmond and Representative Jerrold Nadler saying that they were "deeply disturbed and offended by the language."

The Voice of America, VOA, on January 18, 2018, reported that 78 former US ambassadors to

African countries sent a letter to the White House, expressing "deep concern" over Trump's comments. The statement added in part that "as former US ambassadors to 48 African countries, we write to express our deep concern regarding reports of your recent remarks about African countries and to attest to the importance of our partnerships with most of the 44 African nations."

While lauding entrepreneurs, artists, conversationalists and educators from the continent, the former ambassadors told Trump, "We hope that you will reassess your views on what Africans and African Americans have made and continue to make to our country, our history, and the enduring bonds that will always link Africa and the United States."

More Drastic Measures

Besides just issuing statements, some African countries went a step further in their reaction. Botswana for instance, was reported to have summoned the US Ambassador in that country to clarify what Trump meant in his discourteous statement, just as Nigeria's Minister for Foreign Affairs, Geoffery Onyeama, also summoned US diplomats in the country to explain Trump's remarks, which the minister referred to as "deeply hurtful, offensive and unacceptable."

With the barrage of condemnations from within and outside the African continent, the *"shithole"* furor was deeper than Trump had imagined, especially after failed attempts to deny the demeaning statement. Some others called for an apology from Trump -something he had said during the campaign he did not like doing.

Eventually, Trump bowed to the pressure on him to apologize, and his aides issued a rare apology to African leaders shortly before the 2018 World Economic Forum meeting in Davos, Switzerland. Timed to coincide with the 2018 African Union summit in Ethiopia at the African Union secretariat, Trump, in the January 25, 2018 apology letter, stated, "I want to underscore that the United States deeply respects the people of Africa and my commitment to strong and respectful relationships with African States as sovereign states is firm," Reuters reported.

In the letter, Trump offered his deepest compliments to African leaders, noting that US soldiers were fighting side by side their African counterparts against extremism on the continent and that the US was working to increase free, fair and reciprocal trade with African countries and partnering to safeguard legal infrastructure.

Giving his best wishes for the summit, Trump added that African and US troops were, "fighting side by side to defeat terrorists and build secure communities."

Trump used the apology letter to notify the African leaders that the then United States Secretary of States, Rex Tillerson, would be visiting the continent soon, ostensibly for fence-mending after the slur which had frayed nerves.

CHAPTER THREE

An Untrusted Emissary

As a follow-up to Trump's promise in his rare apology for denigrating the entire black Africa with his *"shithole"* comment, on March 7, 2018, Trump's first Secretary of State, Rex Tillerson, arrived Addis Ababa, Ethiopia, on a five-nation tour of sub-Saharan Africa. Coming after over one year of Trump's assumption of office, Tillerson was the first senior official of Trump administration to visit the region.

The trip was arranged such that the Secretary of State would arrive Addis Ababa during the annual African Union meeting, making it a good rendezvous for African leaders and the US emissary.

Although Tillerson was not a newcomer to Africa, having been combing the entire continent prospecting for crude oil in his former job as Exxon Mobil's chief executive officer, he still had to seek warm reception, going by the circumstances of his visit—soon after an overwhelming condemnation of comment made by his boss, disparaging black African countries.

To get a warm reception in a predictably difficult situation, Tillerson strategically threw an olive branch ahead of his planned trip to avert whatever cold shoulder he might receive, no thanks to the slur language of the US President.

The olive branch could be said to have come in form of a bait that would be irresistible to most of the poor or developing black African countries—financial aid. Suddenly, Trump approved $533 million in humanitarian help to Africa, a sharp turnaround from drastic cuts in financial aid to the region that he had proposed a few months earlier.

It must be noted that it took the intervention of the US Congress to reverse the sharp cuts in financial assistance to Africa proposed by Trump in his very first budget proposals. Trump had proposed cutting US foreign aid to Africa by as much as 35 per cent, from $8 billion to $5.3 billion.

The sudden reversal, from drastic budget cut to aid approval of over half a billion dollars to countries in sub-Saharan Africa, was remarkable. The sudden approval of foreign aid was announced by Tillerson at George Mason University, Virginia, barely hours before he departed for the trip to Ethiopia, Djibouti,

Kenya, Chad and Nigeria, was largely seen as a sweetener to the region by keen followers of the administration's approach to African affairs.

Although widespread condemnations of Trump's uncouth remark on sub-Saharan countries were still on the front burner of US-Africa relations, Tillerson was silent on it while announcing the surprise aid. He instead used the occasion to pledge US commitment to African nations, adding that the Trump administration wanted stronger partnerships on the continent, "with an aim of making African countries more resilient and more self-sufficient."

However, what Tillerson did not tell his audience at George Mason University, while announcing the sudden good gesture of the administration to the region, was that, in the just released National Security Strategy of the Trump administration, there was a proposal to slash funding for the same programs he was trumpeting, along with slashing of other aids seen as vital to Africa, according to reports.

A sudden change in spending pattern in the same budget year and pumping of over half a billion dollars in aid, buttress the fact that Tillerson was on a damage-control mission to Africa, trying to douse the disgust and outrage of Trump's disparagement of an entire continent as made up of *"shithole"* countries.

Fence-Mending Tactics

As an experienced player in the African socio-economic and political environment, Tillerson knew his onions on how to placate the apparently offended African leaders; he knew that praise singing is the name of the game in many parts of the region, especially when over half a billion dollars was being dangled.

Tillerson deployed the praise singing tactic very effectively. Even before he stepped on the continent, while throwing the $533 million aid bait, he showered praises on past successful US programs in Africa and on some leaders responsible for rapid growing economies on the continent.

Said Tillerson: "To understand where the world is going, one must understand that Africa is a significant part of the future," adding, "we're encouraged by the actions of many of our African partners who are seeking ways to expand trade with the United States."

A discerning follower of events is wont to wonder if the gaudy remark is a correct description of a region with "*shithole*" nations. There must have been some fence-mending going on!

During the entire trip, mention was hardly made of Trump's comments, at least in public appearances -

a pointer to the efficacy of the crisis management strategy and tactics deployed.

Not even those at the receiving end of the impudent comments were willing to talk about it anymore. The African leaders made a rather shocking about-face.

Moussa Faki, chairperson of the African Union Commission, who had previously described Trump's comment as conveying contempt, hate and desire to marginalize and exclude Africans, was asked a direct question during a press availability. He pointedly said Trump's Africa remark was in the past!

Tillerson was also asked (twice) during the press conference about the derogatory *"shithole"* remark that Trump had made about Africa in January. He refused to comment.

"The incident is behind us. The visit by the secretary of state today is proof of the importance of relations between the different parties," Faki confirmed.

A Surprising Twist

It can be said that Tillerson did a good job in de-escalating the damage caused by President Trump's indiscretion, especially at the African Union, where it could have become a heated issue. However, the concomitant strain that goes with such reckless demeaning of an entire race can hardly be brushed aside, even by the leaders.

This was even made worse by the sobering fact that the emissary that facilitated the waving aside of the insult, at least by some African leaders, was booted out of office while on the very fence-mending tour - through a tweet message.

On Tuesday, March 13, 2018, President Trump fired his first Secretary of State, Rex Tillerson, with a tweet message, while on the last lap of his trip to Africa. Tillerson had to cut short the five-nation tour and returned to Washington D.C., leaving behind an unfinished business in Africa.

Although the rocky relation between Trump and Tillerson had been public knowledge, as they had reportedly disagreed on many policy issues, the dismissal of Tillerson in such a disgraceful manner for a Secretary of State, puts to question the lifespan of whatever promises and pledges Tillerson must have made on behalf of the administration during the trip.

In the well-publicized speech at George Mason University, where the aid "carrot" had been dangled, shortly before Tillerson's landing on the African soil for the first time as US topmost diplomat, he had said, "I have travelled to North Africa, as I'm sure you'd be aware, but a lot of important countries in East Africa, South Africa, clearly, so obviously this won't be my last trip. I'll have to go back."

As it is now, Tillerson can obviously go back to Africa, but definitely not as the US Secretary of State because, as pointed out by Karen Attiah, Washington Post's Global Editor, "turns out Rex Tillerson's voyage to Africa was the trip of no return."

Empty Shenanigans

Attiah summed up Tillerson's first and last diplomatic trip to Africa and the entire idea behind it this way: "His tenure as Secretary of State is finally ending, but with a whimper. His last hurrah as the top US diplomat came in the form of a half-baked tour to Djibouti, Kenya, Chad, Nigeria and Ethiopia — all key US allies on security and counter-terrorism. He got sick in Kenya and called off the day's activities. He then cut short the Nigeria portion of the trip in order to come home to Washington on to the news that President Trump had fired him and seeks to replace him with CIA Director Mike Pompeo."

Attiah added: "So, what was the point of it all? Couldn't he have just stayed home and send Africa an email? From an optics perspective, the administration no doubt needed to do something to soften the blow of President Trump's "*shithole* countries*" remarks (though Tillerson sidestepped the issue at news conferences), as well as address Trump's nonsensical travel ban on Chad, which fields one of the most dependable fighting forces in West Africa in the fight against Boko Haram. Ultimately, many Africans in the countries he visited were unimpressed."

Going forward, what do the Africans make of a statement like, "I do look forward to returning and building on a strong foundation of US-Africa relations", promised by Rex Tillerson? He apparently cannot do that, having been booted out of office, but has anyone from the administration gone back to either follow up or accomplish that pledge?

Before Trump, former US Presidents worked to build a solid foundation for US-Africa relations. One cannot agree more with Attiah who noted that, "Tillerson's sleepwalker trip was a missed opportunity to signal a new course in the US relations with Africa" under the Trump administration. Not many would be surprise of the missed opportunity, considering Trump's chaotic regime and his depiction of the people in sub-Saharan Africa.

It was, indeed, a lost opportunity because diplomatic observers were so hopeful that the Tillerson trip would be the pedestal from which a meaningful dialogue for an acceptable US-Africa policy would be developed for the administration.

In his contribution to the debate, Brahima Coulibaly, a senior fellow and director of the Africa Growth Initiative at Brookings Institution, shared that optimism writing in the Brookings magazine that "the trip will jumpstart the dialogue that will inform US-Africa policies going forward; also importantly in light of the alleged derogatory comments that President Trump made about Africa. This trip is an opportunity to renew and strengthen longstanding partnerships on the continent."

Besides, Coulibaly, who wrote on "The Trump's Administration's Africa Policy", also pointed out that African observers were upbeat about the trip because, according to him, "since the administration came into office, at least, one of the top three US officials - the President, Vice President and Secretary of State - has visited every global region, except Africa."

Well, at the end of Tillerson's trip of no return, it would be very disconcerting for African policy managers, as well as observers like Coulibaly, that the trip ended in a fiasco, putting US-Africa relations under Trump in a stillborn incubator.

CHAPTER FOUR

US-Africa Relations: From JF Kennedy to Barack Obama

Historically, findings show that there have been a lot of missed opportunities in US-Africa relations. Records show that United States interest in sub-Saharan Africa has always been relatively marginal - not necessarily bound by established positions or strong agreements, as with any other region of the world. Whatever commitment there may be is traced principally to the fact that, at least, 14 percent of the entire US population, according to the 2010 census, trace their ancestry to black Africa.

In 1962, Rupert Emerson wrote in Foreign Affairs magazine that, even though the United States had long been associated with some parts of North Africa, it was very much a newcomer to sub-Saharan Africa. He added that "although the United

States is now being pilloried as the leader among the neo-colonialists, seeking to exploit the newly independent peoples, the actual American stake in Africa is relatively slight."

Writing on "American Policy in Africa", Emerson threw in some figures to substantiate his position then. According to him, in 1960, the whole of the continent took only 4 percent of exports of the United States and supplied only 3.7 percent of American imports. On private investment, the story was much the same. He estimated then that of the $30 billion which Americans invested abroad, less than $850 million was in Africa, contrasting with an American investment of over $10 billion in Canada and more than $8 billion in Latin America.

Admitting at the time that America's investment in Africa was increasing, Emerson noted however that the increase was slow, citing political instability and that "the tendency toward a leftward drift cannot inspire great confidence among foreign investors."

Most pointedly, he noted that, "much of the investment which Africa most gravely needs, and which would prepare the way for other investment, has no charms for the private investor since it concerns such non-profitable spheres as education, health, sanitation, housing, transportation and communications."

This very well explains why, to date, there is more of a preponderance of multilateral institutions and non-governmental bodies from the West in sub-Saharan Africa, than hard core businesses.

Even from a military standpoint, he indicated then that the "US appears to attach no great importance to Africa, save, of course, in terms of the negative consideration that in the cold war era no piece of real estate can be lightly allowed to drift into the hands of the enemy. American bases have been established only in Morocco, Libya and Ethiopia and none exists south of Sahara."

Emerson identified the almost only specific US commitment as the old-standing attachment to Liberia, which, according to him, "dates from the origin of the country as a depository for freed American slaves and [has], in somewhat fitful fashion, been maintained ever since."

As eye-opening as Emerson's write-up is, the most revealing parallel to Trump's labelling of sub-Saharan countries as "*shitholes*" is attributable to one Andrew N. Karmarck.

Karmarck was with the International Bank. In 1958, he wrote thus: "An impressive list of minerals and other raw materials of which Africa is a major supplier can be drawn up, but one is presumably still justified that we could get along without

African commodities and African markets with an imperceptible ripple in our standard of living."

This is quite telling. Although the economic indices stated above have since gone far way up, it can be argued that the mindset about the region, as expressed by Karmack, is still there, now expressed in various subtle ways that may not necessarily be as vocal as that of Trump.

For the numbers, the United States Trade and Investments (USTI), for instance, put total foreign direct investments to sub-Saharan Africa in 2016 at $26 billion. According to USTI, the three largest destinations for U.S. FDI in sub-Sahara Africa were Mauritius ($7.0 billion), South Africa ($5.1 billion), and Nigeria ($3.8 billion). Overall, 60.4 percent of U.S. investment in Africa that year was in the mining sector (which includes crude petroleum), 7.1 percent in manufacturing, and 32.5 percent in other industries (including services and agriculture).

Since then, much more minerals have also been discovered in the region and traded not only with the United States, but also at global markets. But again, to a large extent, the mindset or stereotype about the people and their countries has not changed significantly, a probable reason a sitting US president could make such reported derogatory comments against an entire race.

But the question now is, how did other United States Presidents fare in their relationship with black Africa?

John F. Kennedy

Findings show that except for the men of God (Evangelicals), who took the gospel to what really was then the "uttermost part of the earth", according to the Scripture in Acts 1:8, US-Africa relation was almost non-existent until **President John F. Kennedy** "adopted a more positive and flexible policy toward Africa."

Even then, the motivation, it is gathered, was not in trade or any strategic engagement, but rather the discomforting feeling in the US that all the newly independent African nations exhibited an inclination towards communism.

Therefore, the fundamental American aim is said to have been curtailing communist encroachment on Africa, especially at a time when the arrowheads of communism – USSR (now divided into 15 republics, including Russia) and China - worked to establish themselves as "anti-imperialists and anti-capitalist, uninhibited enemies of colonialism and self-proclaimed protectors of all underdogs not within the communist blog."

To achieve this objective, there was an urgent need to jettison the policy of staying aloof from sub-Saharan Africa. Actions in this new awakening were expedited because, according to America Policy, "the USSR and China have an inescapable appeal to non-white people in the process of breaking loose from the domination of white capitalist empires."

It can therefore be argued that rather than a deep enthusiasm to build a free-enterprise economy and democracy that America is known for, the initial motivation for incursion into sub-Saharan Africa was the protection and spread of an ideology.

Writing in the James Maddison Historical Review, Philip Muehlenbeck stated that President Kennedy was the first American president to make a pointed effort to court African nationalism. According to Muehlenbeck, President Kennedy "did so partly on moral grounds, but strategic considerations were far more important. JFK believed Third World nationalism would become one of the most potent political forces in the second half of the 20th century. In fact, he believed that the growth of Third World nationalism might one day tip the balance of power in the Cold War. For this reason, he made it a priority of his administration to attempt to influence the nationalists of the developing world into aligning with the United States in its global contest against the Soviet Union. He used all means at his disposal

– economic, cultural, personal – to appeal to the leaders of the developing world. Kennedy's focus in this effort centered on Africa, and he set out to court the nationalists of that continent."

Lyndon Johnson

Unlike Kennedy, findings show that President **Lyndon Johnson** did not make very strong footprints in sub-Saharan Africa, but he was said to have been a good supporter of the growing self-determination and swift momentum for independence that was going on in black Africa during his administration. He is reported to have made commitments to help in strengthening regional economic activities like the establishment of the Africa Development Bank, development of 24 colleges and universities, giving scholarships to African students in American universities and financing various communication projects.

Richard Nixon

Exactly two years into his first term, President **Richard Nixon**, on February 18, 1970 precisely, sent to the United States congress a report encapsulating his administration's policy for Africa. The document is reproduced below, unedited:

Africa is a continental experiment in nation building.

The excitement and enthusiasm of national birth have phased into the more sober period of growth.

Our historic ties with Africa are deeply rooted in the cultural heritage of many of our people. Our sympathy for Africa's newly independent states is a natural product of our traditional antipathy for colonialism. Our economic interests in the continent are substantial and growing. And our responsibilities as a global power inevitably give us an interest in the stability and well-being of so large a part of the world.

Reflecting these close ties, Secretary Rogers last year became the first Secretary of State to visit Africa. His personal observations and experiences in Morocco, Tunisia, Ethiopia, Kenya, Zambia, the Congo, Cameroon, Nigeria, Ghana and Liberia gave a new dimension at the highest level to our knowledge and understanding of Africa. A major result of that visit was the basic policy statement issued with my warm approval in March 1970. In that statement Secretary Rogers summarized our aim in Africa as "a relationship of constructive cooperation with the nations of Africa-a cooperative and equal relationship with all who wish it."

We recognize that it is not for us to attempt to set the pattern of relationships among the states of Africa. Only the Africans can forge national unity. Those problems having to do with the building of stable national institutions are neither appropriate for, nor amenable to, much of a contribution from us. Only the Africans themselves can do such work.

The promise of the newly independent African nations is great. But they face all the normal problems associated with independence, and come special ones stemming from historic reliance on tribal organizations not always reflected in national boundaries drawn for the administrative convenience of the former colonial powers. Moreover, colonialism and racial injustice in Southern Africa continue to frustrate the African sense of fulfillment.

These facts complicate the essential task of clothing new political institutions with authority. They make more difficult the problem of working out stable relationships among the nations of Africa, and between Africa and the rest of the world. They compound the exigent task of obtaining and applying the resources needed for economic development.

The Nixon Doctrine's encouragement of self-reliance has an immediate and broad applicability in Africa. Africa has depended less than other areas on American leadership and assistance, and its institutions and relationships were created without our providing either the impetus or the concept. In Africa, therefore, the conflict between the application of our new doctrine and the requirements of continuity are minimal. To an unusual degree, our conception of the current realities is unencumbered by the weight of previous undertakings. Our freedom of decision is not constrained by the demands, legal or implicit, of past commitments and actions.

Within the framework of African efforts, however, there are three primary needs of the continent to which we can contribute. Africa seeks peace, economic development and justice; and she seeks our assistance in reaching those goals. It is in our interest to respond as generously as our resources permit.

U.S. Foreign Policy for the 1970s, Report to the Congress, February 18, 1970

Source: America History-From Revolution to Reconstruction and Beyond.

With widespread nationalism across the African continent during his tenure, the US-Africa relations under President Richard Nixon/Gerald Ford was adherence to the principles that economic development should be the core policy and that respect for African independence and 'nationalism' constitute the foundation of diplomatic relations with sub Saharan countries.

As indicated in the above statement, the Nixon administration made history by being the first to send a top administration official, Secretary of State, to visit the African continent.

Jimmy Carter

The **Jimmy Carter** administration, said to have begun with high hopes, was soon locked in a cold war with the Soviet Union, including escalating confrontations in Africa, South Asia, and Southeast Asia. This largely affected Carter's policies around the globe.

In sub-Saharan Africa, the excitement and enthusiasm for nationalism soon degenerated into authoritarianism, leading to incessant demonstrations and crises.

Essentially, the 1970s in sub-Saharan Africa was characterized by mass unrests. Indeed, no corner of the region was free of upheavals, with some regimes collapsing.

Steve Donoghue wrote in the April 18, 2016 edition of the *Christian Science Monitor* that sub-Saharan Africa was a hotspot, with war between Ethiopia and the Somali Democratic Republic, in the Horn of Africa; as well as the civil war in the country then known as Rhodesia (Zimbabwe).

This is corroborated by Donna Jackson in her book, *Jimmy Carter and the Horn of Africa,* where she pointed out that the crisis in Africa was the first test of Carter's regionalist approach. According to Jackson, "It provoked the very public split between

Secretary of State, Cyrus Vance, and National Security Adviser, Zbigniew Brzezinski, over how to deal with the Soviets, and resulted in a domestic political setback."

In her own collection, titled, *Jimmy Carter in Africa*, Nancy Mitchell stated that "in the waning days of the Ford administration and the first three years of the Carter administration, Africa was the heart of the cold war, Africa was where the superpowers shadow-boxed."

Mitchell, a professor of History at North Carolina State University, in the book, reveals "an administration not beset by weakness and indecision, as is too commonly assumed, but rather constrained by cold war dynamics and by the president's own temperament."

Based on the above, one goes away with the impression that President Carter spent a considerable part of his tenure fighting the cold war, with sub-Saharan Africa caught in the middle, as he waged the United States-led war on communism.

Ronald Reagan

Whatever footprints President **Ronald Reagan** made in sub-Saharan Africa was obviously overshadowed by his rather dogmatic "constructive engagement" policy in dismantling the apartheid regime in South Africa. Reports say it took the intervention of the US Congress to override the controversial policy, in order to make way for the collapse of the oppressive apartheid regime.

Peter Krogh (Peter Frederic) of Georgetown University, School of Foreign Service, wrote that "for the first five years of the Reagan administration, the United States pursued a policy of 'constructive engagement' with South Africa government, believing that positive diplomatic relations would pave the way for reform of its repressive apartheid system."

According to Krogh, although some economic gains were made during this period, "political rights remained scarce, and by 1985 a campaign was growing in the United States that called for a tougher stance on apartheid. Leading the charge for this movement on Capitol Hill was the Conservative Opportunity Society, a group of young Republican congressmen pushing for increased opposition to apartheid."

Notwithstanding complaints from within the United States and elsewhere that the constructive engagement policy was benefiting the apartheid regime, President Reagan is said to have maintained his stance. He based his policy on two premises:

one, the insistence that regional peacemaking in South Africa was the necessary precondition for change within South Africa. This is said to have included such extraneous issues as the Cuban troops' withdrawal from Angola.

The second was his conviction that the South Africa President, Pieter Botha and his generals were genuinely capable of reforming apartheid, and in fact were committed to doing just that, reports say.

However, Sean Jacobs, Editor, *Africa is a Country*, noted that "the 1980s became the most bloody decade in the region's history, as the South African government, backed by the US, pursued proxy-wars in Angola and Mozambique, fomented conflict between local groups inside these states, conducted commando raids into Botswana, hunting for members of the anti-apartheid resistance and occupied Namibia - in the process, killing and displacing thousands of people, militarizing whole populations and crippling economic systems."

Jacobs pointed out that "when Botha unleashed full scale state terror in the aftermath of his now-infamous Rubicon speech (where he reneged on promised reforms) in 1985, Reagan instead blamed South Africa's deepening political and economic crises on the African National Congress (ANC) and "tribalism". When the US Congress finally succeeded in enacting stringent sanctions against the South African regime and businesses, largely through popular pressure, they met strong resistance from the White House: Reagan first vetoed, then reluctantly implemented the measures."

In the middle of the incidents, it is worth noting that the press called out the infamous constructive engagement, but to no avail. In the Washington Post article reproduced below, Philip Geyelin traced the birth of the dysfunctional constructive engagement policy and correctly forecasted its fate:

Understanding Reagan's Policy

As a practical political matter, "constructive engagement" in South Africa is no longer a winning formulation for U.S. policy in South Africa. But before we pronounce it dead, we ought to be clear in our minds what it is we want to bury -- the contents or the label?

If it's the label, fine. "Constructive engagement" has long since joined the list of catchwords for one or another piece of foreign policy that have been bent out of shape by loose usage for this or that political purpose ("containment," "d,etente," "linkage," "massive retaliation"). For lack of an effective administration defense in the face of mounting violence and brutal repression by South Africa's white supremacists, "constructive engagement" has become a code word for a policy designed purely and simply to "dismantle" the system of apartheid by the pusillanimous practice of quiet diplomacy. From this it is no big jump to the conclusion that "constructive engagement" was always a wicked wink at the evils of apartheid out of concern for South Africa as a strategic asset.

Hence the cries for a radical departure from the old Reagan policy to something fundamentally new. The result is a) an overwrought and rancid debate between a needlessly defensive administration and a Democratic opposition overreaching for partisan gain, and b) precisely the wrong signal to be sending to Pretoria.

Forget the label and reexamine the original contents of "constructive engagement." You will find that, as between the recommended new departures and the "old policy," there is not all that much to fight about.

The roots of "constructive engagement" are to be found in an article in the 1980-81 issue of Foreign Affairs magazine by Chester A. Crocker, then the director of African studies at the Center for Strategic and International Studies at Georgetown University and soon to be assistant secretary of state for African affairs and the prime mover of African policy in the Reagan administration. "Constructive engagement" was actually offered as an antidote to the Nixon administration's conduct of South African policy "in the closet" -- to a "de facto acquiescence in the policies of

Pretoria." But Crocker clearly intended "constructive engagement" as a formula for dealing not just with South Africa but with blacks and whites "in the region as a whole." It was aimed at promoting general stability and containing violence. As for South Africa, its government was to be constructively engaged not only on behalf of "evolutionary change toward a non-racial system" at home but in the interests of independence for Namibia, the removal of Cuban troops from Angola, and an effort to eliminate causes of tension and hostility in the whole neighborhood.

If there was anything genuinely innovative about Crocker's thinking, as it was later incorporated into Reagan administration policy, it was not so much in its substantive departure from past U.S. policy as in the tactics and priorities. It was in his attempt to define limits as well as potential -- to ration the influence he thought the United States could reasonably hope to bring to bear.

Ironically, the bitterest opposition in his nomination proceedings came from Sen. Jesse Helms, who saw Crocker as a dangerous "elitist," peddling a brand of "egalitarianism" that would lead to a "surrender" by South African whites, allowing them to "retain their lives, and perhaps their property but not their power or their culture."

Now you can argue that Crocker's concept has been

imperfectly applied. Surely the administration has been slow to deal with internal pulling and hauling over how hard to push Pretoria. But that's not an argument for a whole new policy. What is really needed is a more constructive understanding in Congress of the policy we have in place.

By Philip Geyelin
The Washington Post
September 20, 1985

The Reagan administration also offered covert support to the Jonas Savimbi-led National Union for the Total Independence of Angola (UNITA) against the communist-led People's Movement for the Liberation of Angola (MPLA).

Reports say Savimbi was strongly supported by Heritage Foundation and visited with Reagan in 1986 in the White House, during which Reagan spoke of UNITA winning the war.

George H. Bush

It is common knowledge that President **George H. Bush** focused more on foreign affairs during his presidency. But what was his approach to US-Africa relations?

During his single-term presidency, President Bush, unlike his reluctant predecessor, helped speed up the dismantling of the apartheid system of government in South Africa by supporting sanctions imposed by the United States Congress against the South African government.

On July 17, 1991 his administration lifted the sanctions, saying that the movement to end apartheid was now "irreversible."

Towards the end of his tenure, faced with a humanitarian disaster in Somalia, due to a breakdown in civil order, Bush sent US troops to the country to help restore order and ease the humanitarian crisis of drought, famine and starvation, in line with United Nations mission, tagged, "Operation Restore Hope".

Herman J. Cohen, Bush's assistant secretary of state for Africa affairs, stated recently that President Bush found Africa worthy of his attention.

Writing in *The Hill* edition of December 06, 2018, Cohen stated that Bush would always say "there is no reason why Africans and their governments can't do as well as people in the other regions."

According to Cohen, Bush understood Africa's potential, as well as the basis for its struggles. In particular, Cohen added that "Bush supported financing democracy and good governance programs in Africa, but our emphasis was on conflict resolution: he saw that there could be no progress in development while wars cut all of the gains."

Bush's hands-on approach, Cohen pointed out, led to a number of outstanding successes in the drive to end Africa's conflicts, an approach that saw him working to bring peace in Ethiopia, Angola and Mozambique, including of course, the end of the apartheid regime in South Africa.

Bill Clinton

No United States President has focused so early on sub-Saharan Africa like President **Bill Clinton** did. This was not really because the region was a top priority of his administration, but because necessity was placed upon him to immediately follow up on the actions of his predecessor.

Professor Russell Riley of the Miller Center, University of Virginia, aptly described the situation: "Barely few weeks before Clinton took office, outgoing President George H. Bush, had sent American troops into Somalia. What started out as a humanitarian mission to combat famine grew into a bloody military struggle, with the bodies of dead American soldiers dragged through the streets of the Somalian capital of Mogadishu in October 1993."

Consequent upon this gruesome development, public support for the American mission waned in the US and Clinton had no choice but to announce, in March 1994, a full withdrawal of US forces from Somalia.

So devastating was the brutal killing of the US soldiers that the Clinton administration became hesitant to immediately engage in any other peace-keeping mission. As such, when the Rwandan genocide began soon after, the US paid no attention. This gave room for the unprecedented massacre reportedly perpetuated by the government in power, killing over 800,000 people, mainly the Tutsis. Several years later, reports say, Clinton remarked that his refusal to intervene in the carnage was among his biggest regrets as president.

Even with the involuntary initial entry into Africa affairs, historians say the Clinton years saw an unusual high-level United States engagement in Africa, "and the articulation of a vision of partnership based on consultation and ambitious policy initiatives," according to J. Stephen Morris.

Some of the initiatives and accomplishments of the Clinton administration in sub-Saharan Africa are listed to include amongst others:

• Hosted the first-ever White House conference on Africa in July 1994. This conference brought together key American policy-makers and leaders to discuss the future of US-Africa relations.

- Made a historic presidential trip to Africa. In 1998, President Clinton made the first trip by a sitting US President to Ghana, Uganda, Botswana and Senegal. While in Africa, President Clinton focused on key issues of development, trade, investment, empowerment of women and the environment. The trip increased and enhanced ties with Africa and built upon the work and achievements of late Commerce Secretary, Ron Brown; Transportation Secretary, Slater; and Presidential Special Envoy, Jesse Jackson.

- Assisted South Africa's transition to democracy. Provided over $600 million in the first three years to the newly-elected democratic government of South Africa to support democracy and development. Established the Gore-Mbeki Bi-National Commission to promote cooperation in trade, development, the environment and security.

- Launched the President's Partnership for Economic Opportunity in Africa Initiative. This initiative was to deepen trade and investment between Africa and the United States and was the cornerstone of the Administration's Africa policy. (Source: Clinton White Archives)

In addition, Clinton created the African Growth and Opportunity Act (AGOA) signed into law in May 2000, with the objective of expanding U.S. trade and investment with sub-Saharan Africa, to stimulate economic growth, encourage economic integration, and specifically facilitate sub-Saharan Africa›s integration into the global economy.

Since its enactment in 2000, AGOA has been at the core of US economic policy and commercial engagement with Africa. AGOA provided eligible sub-Saharan African countries with duty-free access to the US market for over 1,800 products, in addition to the more than 5,000 products that are eligible for duty-free access under the Generalized System of Preferences program.

Although critics spotlight missed opportunities in AGOA, but by providing new market opportunities, AGOA is said to have helped bolster economic growth, promoted economic and political reform, and improved U.S. economic relations in the sub-Saharan region.

- According to statistics from the AGOA website, as at 2018, 40 countries in sub Saharan Africa were eligible for AGOA benefits.

- AGOA Recent Trade and Investment Statistics

- Total two-way goods trade between the United States and sub-Saharan Africa increased 5.8%, from $36.9 billion in 2015 to $39 billion in 2017.

- Top U.S. goods exports to sub-Saharan Africa: machinery ($2.3 billion), vehicles ($1.6 billion), aircraft ($1.5 billion), mineral fuels ($1.4 billion), and electrical machinery ($864 million).

- Top U.S. export markets in the region: South Africa ($5 billion), Nigeria ($2.2 billion), Ghana ($886 million), Ethiopia ($873 million), and Angola ($810 million).

- Top U.S. imports from sub-Saharan Africa: oil ($11.2 billion), precious metals ($4.1 billion), cocoa ($1.2 billion), vehicles ($1.2 billion), and iron and steel ($950 million)

- Top sub-Saharan African suppliers to the United States were South Africa ($7.8 billion), Nigeria ($7.1 billion), Angola ($2.6 billion), Cote d'Ivoire ($1.2 billion), and Botswana ($772 million).

- U.S. investment in sub-Saharan Africa stood at $29 billion in 2016, the latest year available, down 23%, compared to $37.5 billion in 2014. The three largest destinations for U.S. investment were Mauritius ($6.7 billion), South Africa ($5.1 billion) and Nigeria ($3.8 billion).

- Sub-Saharan Africa foreign direct investment in the U.S. stood at $4.2 billion in 2016, up 164%, compared to $1.6 billion in 2014.

It could therefore be said, without mincing words, that the Clinton years saw unprecedented high-level engagement in Africa and the articulation of a vision of partnership, based on consultation and ambitious policy initiatives.

George W. Bush

It is on record that, so far, no United States president, living or dead, has impacted sub-Saharan Africa as President **George W. Bush.** Even some of Bush's most ardent critics admit that his foreign policy legacy on Africa continues to have a lasting effect.

The US-Africa relations under his watch witnessed unparalleled partnerships strengthened democracies, poverty alleviation and life-saving interventions. A good testimony of these feats was given by a fellow US President during the Bush presidential library dedication in April 2013, which brought together five living Presidents of the United States.

At that event, President Jimmy Carter said, "Mr. President, let me say that I'm filled with admiration for you and deep gratitude for you about the great contributions you've made to the most needy people on earth."

An attempt to chronicle George W. Bush's footprint in sub-Saharan Africa shows an impressive list of accomplishments.

According to documents from the White House, between 1988 and 2007, under the Bush administration, the United States dramatically increased its commitment to development in Africa – and transformed the way it was carried out. Some of the accomplishments are:

* The United States partnered with African leaders to empower Africans to overcome poverty by growing their economies.

  Under the leadership of President Bush, the U.S. delivered historic aid increases to Africa. In President Bush's first term, the United States more than doubled development assistance to Africa – part of the largest expansion of American development assistance since the Marshall Plan.

  President Bush pledged to increase total assistance (both bilateral and multilateral) to $8.7 billion by 2010, double the size of 2004 levels. The President's FY 2009 budget request, combined with previous budgets and program implementation, ensured that the United States met the important commitment.

- President Bush secured international agreement on the Multilateral Debt Relief Initiative. This Initiative provided 100 percent debt relief from the major international financial institutions to the world's poorest, most heavily indebted countries. It reduced a total of $42 billion in debt – $34 billion of which was for 19 African countries. Over time, a total of 33 African countries would receive full debt relief. The U.S. also secured reforms with the international financial institutions aimed at preventing the re-accumulation of unsustainable debt.

- Bush launched the Millennium Challenge Account as a new model to support governments that commit to ruling justly, investing in people, and encouraging economic freedom. The Millennium Challenge Corporation (MCC) signed at least seven compacts with African countries totaling $2.4 billion to fight poverty through economic growth.

- The President worked with Congress to extend the African Growth and Opportunity Act (AGOA). Thanks in part to AGOA, over 98 percent of African exports to the US entered the U.S. duty-free. In 2007, AGOA exports to the U.S. totaled over $50 billion – more than six times the level in 2001, the first full year of

AGOA. During the same period, U.S. exports to sub-Saharan Africa have doubled, totaling over $14 billion.

- In May 2007, President Bush announced the Africa Financial Sector Initiative and created seven new investment funds that mobilized more than $1.6 billion through support of OPIC. This was to strengthen financial markets, mobilize domestic and foreign investment, and help spur job creation and economic growth. Also, OPIC supported several investment funds that mobilized roughly $1.3 billion in private investment for the continent.

- In 2006, President Bush launched the African Global Competitiveness Initiative (AGCI), to provide $200 million over five years in support of increased trade and investment in Africa. Four regional Global Competitiveness Hubs were the primary implementers of AGCI and were located in Ghana and Senegal for West Africa, Botswana for Southern Africa and Kenya for East and Central Africa.

Over the last seven years of the Bush administration, the US committed $1.6 billion of trade capacity building assistance to sub-Saharan Africa, including $505 million in FY 2007 alone. This assistance was intended to help African governments reduce barriers to trade and for African businesses, workers, and farmers to benefit more fully from global trade.

- Partnership to alleviate hunger, expand education, and fight disease. During the Bush administration, the United States' humanitarian food aid totaled more than $1.7 billion in FY 2007, and emergency food aid reached about 23 million people in 30 countries.

- In 2006, the United States provided $195 million – the first year of a five-year effort – to support the African Union's Comprehensive African Agricultural Development Program. This program promoted the critical role of agricultural development as a means to eliminate hunger, reduce poverty and food insecurity, increase trade, and promote wealth in Africa.

- To help African countries feed their own people, the President called on Congress to support his proposal to use a portion of US food aid funding to purchase crops directly from farmers in Africa, instead of shipping in food assistance from the developed world. This initiative was aimed at building up local agriculture markets and help break the cycle of famine.

- In 2002, President Bush launched the Africa Education Initiative (AEI) and committed to provide $600 million over eight years to increase access to quality basic education. By 2010, AEI had distributed over 15 million textbooks, trained nearly one million teachers, and provided 550,000 scholarships for girls.

- In May 2007, President Bush also announced the President's Expanded Education for the World's Poorest Children and committed an additional $525 million over five years for education improvement. This initiative was to provide over four million children with access to quality basic education in six target countries, four of which were in Africa -Ethiopia, Ghana, Liberia, and Mali -and supported after-school skills development programs.

- In 2003, President Bush launched the President's Emergency Plan for AIDS Relief (PEPFAR), committing $15 billion over five years to combat global HIV/AIDS. PEFPAR remains the largest international health initiative in history to fight a single disease. Through this program, the US partnered with local African communities and organizations, including faith- and community-based organizations, to support HIV/AIDS treatment, care, and prevention activities.

- In 2007, PEPFAR supported life-saving anti-retroviral treatment for over 1.3 million people in sub-Saharan Africa alone, up from 50,000 when the President last visited Africa in 2003.

• On May 30, 2007, President Bush announced his proposal to double America's initial commitment and provide an additional $30 billion over the next five years. The President then called on Congress to pass reauthorizing legislation that maintains PEPFAR›s successful founding principles.

Before then in 2005, President Bush launched the President's Malaria Initiative (PMI), committing $1.2 billion over five years to reduce malaria deaths by 50 percent in 15 target African countries. The President challenged the private sector to join the fight against malaria, and it was estimated that the PMI had already reached 25 million people in Sub-Saharan Africa.

The United States under Bush's watch became the largest contributor to the Global Fund for HIV/AIDS, malaria, and tuberculosis, pledging more than $3.5 billion and providing over $2.5 billion since 2001.

America's charitable organizations served on the frontlines with African faith-based and community groups to advance health, education and development goals. PEPFAR, PMI, and other US-funded efforts represented massive-scale implementation of the Bush's vision for his faith-based and community Initiative by empowering these organizations in their determined attack on need.

Partnership to empower Africans end conflicts, strengthen democracy, and promote peace.

President Bush's partnership with allies, regional leaders, and sub-regional organizations led to the ending of wars in Liberia, Sierra Leone, Sudan (north-south), Democratic Republic of the Congo (DRC), Angola, and Burundi.

America continued to work closely with local partners to address remaining security challenges in Africa.

Darfur: In the case of Darfur, the United States continued to deliver humanitarian assistance, enforced sanctions against Sudanese government officials, rebel leaders, and others responsible for violence, and call this killing what it is – genocide.

Eastern Congo: In Eastern Congo, agreements were brokered with leaders on the ground to demobilize all remaining armed groups.

Kenya: In Kenya, there was a call for there to be an immediate halt to the violence, justice for the victims of abuse, and a full return of democracy. The President asked Secretary of State Condoleezza Rice to travel to Kenya to support the work of the former Secretary General Kofi Annan.

America also stood with all in Africa who live under tyranny. President Bush urged neighbors in the region – including South Africa – to work for an end to the suffering in Zimbabwe, where a discredited dictator presided over food shortages, staggering inflation, and harsh repression.

Within two years 2005-2007, the United States trained over 39,000 African peacekeepers in 20 countries. The US trained over 80 percent of African peacekeepers who were deployed in African Union and United Nations missions, both inside and outside of Africa, and also partnered with the AU and member states to support the establishment of an African Standby Force.

The United States, under President Bush, was dedicated to promoting democracy and human rights and assisting refugees in Africa. In four years alone, there were more than 50 democratic elections in Africa, and in more than two-thirds of sub-Saharan African nations. President Bush supported democratic transitions in many African countries, such as Liberia and Mauritania; strengthened democratic institutions in post-conflict countries, such as the DRC and Burundi; and assisted civil society organizations across Africa in combating gender-based violence, trafficking in persons, and other human rights violations. In FY 2007, the US provided close to $175 million for programs to promote just and democratic governance in African nations.

The United States, under Bush, was the largest donor to the Office of the United Nations High Commissioner for Refugees (UNHCR), with more than 40 percent of that funding going to Africa in 2007.

The interesting aspect of President Bush's strong engagement with sub-Saharan Africa is that it is widely acknowledged. Bob Geldof wrote in Time Magazine, May 3, 2008 edition, that Africa is the "triumph of America foreign policy and is the Bush administration's greatest achievement."

Teresa Welsh, staff writer with US News wrote in 2015 that "with only 17 months remaining in his term, Obama has yet to achieve any real policy victories in Africa. And as he has struggled to balance a full plate of crises in other parts of the world, the accomplishments of the nation's first African-American president appear noticeably thinner than those of his predecessor, former President George W. Bush."

From the Center for Global Development, two experts on Africa, Amanda Glassman and Jenny Ottenhoff commented that "PEPFAR has helped changed the equation on what was once — not too long ago — seen as an insurmountable plague."

Shortly before Bush left office, he did more. He announced some new steps to help continue the progress he has made on America-Africa relations, including:

- Adding five investment funds, supported by the Overseas Private Investment Corporation (OPIC). These funds would mobilize $875 million in capital for the continent. This was in addition to $750 million in investment capital that would be mobilized by OPIC Funds previously announced by the administration, bringing the total to more than $1.6 billion.

- During his trip to sub-Saharan Africa, Bush signed the largest project in the Millennium Challenge Corporation's history – a $698 million dollar compact with Tanzania. This Compact was planned to benefit 4.8 million Tanzanians.

- A bilateral investment treaty was signed with Rwanda, first of such treaty in sub-Saharan Africa in a decade. The treaty promoted investment by providing legal protections for US and Rwandan investors that underscore the two countries› shared commitment to open investment and trade policies.

John Seven of History publication, stated that "much of the legacy of President George Bush is wrapped around the war on terror and military action in Iraq and Afghanistan, but what many consider his greatest achievement is a public health effort steeped in humanitarianism that won accolades across the political spectrum. Bush has probably done more than any other president to combat AIDS, particularly in Africa."

But more importantly however, at least for this book, is President George Bush's perception of the sub-Saharan region.

Discussing his trip to Africa at the Leon H. Sullivan Foundation, on February 26, 2008, Bush said: *"America is on a mission of mercy, we are treating African leaders as equal partners. We expect them to produce measurable results. We expect them to fight corruption and invest in the health and education of their people and pursue market-based economic policies. This mission serves our moral interests—we are all children of God and having the power to save lives comes with the obligation to use it."*

On that very day and occasion, President Bush added: *"Americans should feel proud, mighty proud, of the work we are doing in Africa. At every stop, I told people that the source of all these efforts is the generosity of the American people. We are a nation of compassionate and good-hearted folks. We recognize the extraordinary potential of Africa."*

Underscoring the motivation for his policy approach to Africa, Bush said: *"Too many nations continue to follow either the paternalistic notion that treats African countries as charity cases, or a model of exploitation that seeks to buy their resources. America rejects both approaches. The United*

States is treating the leaders of Africa as equal partners, asking them to set clear goals, and expecting them to produce measurable results. Together, Africa's leaders and the United States are working to pioneer a new era in development on African continent."

Barack Obama

Being the first African-American President of the United States, there were very high expectations that President Barack Obama would leave an indelible legacy in Africa. However, after the eight years of his two-term presidency, keen observers of his tenure say it is not necessarily so, although his admirers argue time will tell better.

At a panel discussion hosted by the Africa Security Initiative on July 19, 2016, with the topic, "What Legacy Will Obama Leave on the Continent?" participants were of the consensus that "the effects of Obama's legacy in Africa have not yet been fully manifested."

Writing in the Brookings publication, Ian Livingston indicated that the participants at the panel discussion concluded that barely few months to the end of Obama's presidency, *"the fact that Barack Obama was the first African-American elected to be president in the US history will not make his legacy in Africa particularly historic."*

With four trips to Africa, the most by any United States president, spanning six sub-Saharan countries: Ghana, Senegal, Ivory Coast, Ethiopia, Kenya and South Africa, Livingston believes the trips reflect Obama's "belief in the continent's importance, even if he arguably hasn't been able to devote the resources he might have wished, given the myriad of competing demands."

Professor Matthew Carotenuto, of St. Lawrence University and author of *Obama and Kenya: Contested Histories and the Politics of Belonging,* pointed out at the discussion program that "Obama's relationship with Africa is particularly challenging because of his Kenyan heritage," noting that Obama was sensitive to charges of favoritism and to critiques that he might be too focused on the continent of his relatives and his late father.

That, notwithstanding, Sarah Margon, Washington director at Human Rights Watch highlighted what she listed as some strengths and weaknesses of Obama's policy in Africa.

As pointed out by Livingston, strengths, in Margon's view, include that the Obama administration:

• Improved governance and democracy through strong messaging;

- Balanced counterterrorism and civil rights, without letting the former dominate the latter;

- Made human rights and LGBT issues a clear priority;

- Carried out the Africa Leader's Summit and the "Power Africa" electricity initiative, with modestly promising results; and

- Used social media to engage local populations.

On the other hand, Margon is of the opinion that Obama's administration showed weakness, when it:

- Focused on security assistance in ways that gave somewhat less priority to governance issues at times, at least in terms of U.S. financial resources, and aligned the United States with authoritarian regimes in several cases;

- Provided inconsistent follow-up towards crisis response in Guinea, Nigeria, and the Central African Republic, among other places; and

- Failed to hold governments accountable for human rights violations in places like Ethiopia.

There is indeed a growing sentiment that Obama did not do much for black Africa. Take, for instance, the earlier referenced statement by Teresa Welsh, staff writer with US News, who wrote in 2015 that "with only 17 months remaining in his term, Obama has yet to achieve any real policy victories in Africa. And as he has struggled to balance a full plate of crises in other parts of the world, the accomplishments of the nation's first African-American president appear noticeably thinner than those of his predecessor, former President George W. Bush."

But Peter Pham, director of the Atlantic Council's Africa Center, thinks otherwise. In an opinion article he penned for Newsweek magazine in August 2016, Pham stated that "President Obama's legacy in Africa is a state of mind."

According to Pham, "If the Obama legacy does not include signature initiatives comparable to the enactment of the African Growth and Opportunity Act (AGOA) under President Bill Clinton or the creation of the United States Africa Command (AFRICOM)—the US military headquarters for the continent—by President George W. Bush, it would be a mistake to discount the change that has occurred during Obama's watch."

Writing for the BBC on "Barack Obama: How will Africa Remember Him?', Nancy Kacungira stated that "Trade, not aid" was the cornerstone of US policy for Africa under Mr. Obama, a point Obama himself emphasized in an interview with the BBC in 2015 saying, "People are not interested in just being patrons or being patronized and being given aid - they're interested in building capacity".

In terms of signature initiatives, the Obama administration launched three major business initiatives:

- Power Africa, a $7 billion program to develop Africa's energy sector by providing technical assistance, financing and investment support.

- Trade Africa, a program to bolster intra-regional and global trade, meant to expand trade agreements, reduce barriers, and increase competitiveness among many of Africa's leading economies.

- The Young African Leaders Initiative YALI, hailed as Obama's initiative in Africa to build leadership skills of young Africans through exchange programs with the United States.

For many observers, Obama's engagement and attention to Africa during his first term in office was disappointing. Records show that Obama's engagement with Africa started towards the end of his first term in office when his administration issued the U.S. Strategy toward sub-Saharan Africa on June 14, 2012.

The strategy was based on four pillars of engagement with sub-Saharan Africa. These include:

(1) strengthening democratic institutions; (2) spurring economic growth, trade, and investment; (3) advancing peace and security; and (4) promoting opportunity and development.

Dereje Seyoum, a research officer at the Africa Peace and Security Program, is of the opinion that, in some cases, the impact of Obama's engagement in Africa is yet to be reaped. For instance, he is of the opinion that the former President's impacts through the Young African Leaders Initiatives will be seen in the decades to come than the immediate tomorrow.

Although coming late, nearly halfway in his presidential term, Seyoum noted that Obama did the most in securing and advancing US-Africa relations. The different initiatives started under the Obama administration will serve as anchors for future US engagement in Africa. But whether future administration will build on that is another matter altogether, especially as Trump, his immediate successor takes pride in dismantling Obama projects.

People say Obama's policy toward sub-Saharan Africa was centered on trade and investment, different from that of Bush who focused on health, education and humanitarian assistance, but it can be argued as pointed out by Kacungira, that the substance of Obama's presidency may not have been what many Africans had hoped for, but surely, its symbolism remains strong.

In assessing his relationship with Africa, as President of United States, Obama himself told the BBC that "we must start from the simple premise that Africa's future is up to Africans." That is also telling and a discussion for another day.

CHAPTER FIVE

The Murky Story of Foreign Aid

Africa's future may indeed be up to Africans, but in life's journey, success is often determined by the level of help one gets, since no man is an island. Black Africa sure needs help, and it would be remiss not to include the issue of foreign aid in any discussion on development in sub-Saharan Africa. This is because foreign aid has fortuitously become a staple source of income for many societies on the continent. It therefore makes foreign aid a topical issue at any forum on economic development in the region.

In recent years, however, there has been a growing debate on the efficacy or otherwise of foreign aid to sub-Saharan African countries. Those against foreign aid say that it is hurting, rather than helping, sub-Saharan African countries. Conversely, foreign aid advocates maintain that it is indispensable in tackling poverty.

While the aim of this chapter is not to go into the intricacies and measurable impacts of foreign aid to the region, or who gives what to whom, it is apt to point out that the objectives of foreign aid are generally very noble and laudable. It is also pertinent to indicate that donors give aid for diverse reasons and the objectives of foreign aid could be covert or overt. For instance, as the cold war developed, super powers used aid to encourage political allegiances and strategic advantages with their allies to gain leverage at the comity of nations.

Victoria Williams, an expert on foreign aids, expands on this, explaining that it could be used to prevent friendly governments from falling under the influence of unfriendly ones, or as payment for the right to establish or use military bases on foreign soil. According to Williams, "Foreign aid also may be used to achieve a country's diplomatic goals, enabling it to gain diplomatic recognition, to garner support for its positions in international organizations, or to increase its diplomats' access to foreign officials.

"Other purposes of foreign aid include promoting a country's exports (e.g., through programs that require the recipient country to use the aid to purchase the donor country's agricultural products or manufactured goods) and spreading its language, culture, or religion. Countries also provide aid to relieve suffering caused by natural or man-made disasters, such as famine, disease, war; to promote economic development; as well as to help establish or strengthen political institutions and address a variety of transnational problems, including disease, terrorism and other crimes, including destruction of the environment."

But whether the aforementioned benefits of foreign aid have always been accomplished is another matter altogether. To some people, if the aid is a short-term relief for crisis, such as starvation, environmental disasters, epidemic, etc., it is worth it because, to them, there is an undeniable moral imperative for humanitarian organizations to give aid and lessen immediate suffering.

But when it is for poverty alleviation or socio-economic development, analysts say that foreign aid has fallen short. This group of analysts maintain that aid distribution over the years has left developing countries in a worse state than before the aid. Writing in the journal, *Le Journal International Archives,* Juliette Lyons says that "when we take a look at the statistics of foreign aid budgets to Chad, Angola or Nigeria, the level of progress suddenly appears to be very low when compared to the huge sums received.

Lyons added in her research findings that "the continent as a whole receives roughly $50 billion of international assistance annually, yet, instead of drastically improving the living conditions of the 600 million people who live below poverty line, aid makes the rich richer, the poor poorer and hinders economic growth in the region."

Globally, millions of poor people are reported to have moved out of abject poverty in the last six decades, but keen followers of the aid business say it has had little to do with foreign aid, but instead largely due to sustained economic management growth in places like Asia, for example, which receives little or no aid.

According to the World Bank, between 1981 and 2010, the number of poor people globally fell by 700 million; and in China alone, with relatively no aid assistance, the number of poor people fell by 627 million or 98.6 per cent. Analysts opposed to foreign aid quickly jumped at the World Bank research findings to support their long-held argument that, to a large extent, foreign aid does not move people out of poverty.

Analysts, such as Daron Acemoglu and James Robinson, in their article, "Why Foreign Aid Fails: And How to Really Help Africa," point out that "more than a quarter of countries in sub-Saharan

Africa are poorer today than in 1960, with no sign that foreign aid, however substantive, will end poverty in the region."

Instead of ending poverty, the authors say foreign aid strengthens corruption, especially in countries where there is endemic corruption, a fact corroborated by Lyons that, "unfortunately this is the case for many of the countries that make up sub-Saharan Africa."

Transparency International buttresses the above assertion, adding that the largest recipients of foreign aid are in sub-Saharan Africa, home to the world's lowest ranked countries in many areas of governance, especially in terms of corruption.

Lyons reveals from her study that "foreign aid simply reinforces the amount of resources available to already corrupt specific elite groups of people." There is, she indicated, a clear correlation between increased aid and statistically significant increase in corruption.

Her argument is that the money from foreign aid is not distributed evenly among the population or used to promote growth and to help the poor, but instead used on military equipment, white elephant projects and dishonest procurements. It is also used by leaders who are short of time with policies and want to achieve them quickly, by increasing the size of the government with civil servants to cut down the unemployment rate.

Acemoglu and Robinson are even more specific, using Angola as an example. According to their article, to understand Angola's endemic poverty, one should consider the country's richest woman, Isabel dos Santos, billionaire daughter of the former president, Jose Eduardo dos Santos who served from 1979 to 2017. The analysts cite a recent investigation by Forbes magazine into her fortune, which concluded that "as best as we can trace, every major Angolan investment held by dos Santos stems either from taking a chunk of a company that wants to do business in the country or from a stroke of the president's pen that cut her into the action."

Regrettably, according to the article, she did this, when the World Bank said only a quarter of Angolans had access to electricity in 2009 and a third were living on incomes of less than $2 a day.

This demonstrates, the article indicated, that "aid to Angola is likely to help the president's daughter rather than the average citizen."

Besides feeding corruption, critics say foreign aid also fosters dependency, where country leaders idle around, waiting for foreign aid without initiating strategic home-grown policies that could generate income.

Be that as it may, findings carried out show that the well-oiled aid industry has thrived for decades and operators are not thinking of closing shop anytime soon, despite growing criticism.

This is not in any way to underestimate the beneficial role of foreign aid. There is without a doubt, an undeniable need for well-meaning organizations to get involved in providing aid for those in one type of crisis or the other.

The argument rather, is that instances abound to prove that foreign aid feeds corruption and fosters dependency. Going forward, analysts recommend that foreign aid should be less about giving out money, but more about collegial engagement of donors and recipients of aid to achieve the desired objectives.

A better way forward is the use of government functionaries and or machinery as middle-men to manage foreign aid on behalf of the needy should be eliminated. This is because, in many African countries replete with poverty-stricken individuals and households, the funds develop wings and fly before they get to the intended recipients.

CHAPTER SIX

China in Africa

In engaging with Africa, some countries have carefully navigated their ways beyond giving foreign aid. One of such is China. The narrative that China's growing presence in Africa is exploitative and dysfunctional may make a good talking point to either new entrants into the discourse or those that have never set their foot on any black African country. Whether good or bad, the fact on ground is that China has a noticeable domineering presence in sub-Saharan Africa.

Over the years, China had worked so hard and eventually succeeded in becoming the largest economic partner, both in trade and in foreign direct investment in the region; and it is growing.

Economic ties between China and Africa, especially sub-Saharan Africa, have deepened, as China surpassed the United States to become Africa's largest trade partner in 2009. Currently, China is a destination for 15 to 16 per cent of sub-Saharan Africa's exports and the source of 14 to 21 percent of the region's imports, according to estimates from the World Bank.

The People's Bank of China, China Development Bank, the Export-Import Bank of China and the China-Africa Development Fund are some of the creditors of these loans and investigations show that Ethiopia, Kenya and Sudan are the top recipients so far.

Between 2000 and 2015, Chinese banks, contractors, and the government loaned more than $94.4 billion to Africa, according to John Hopkins School of Advanced and International Studies and the China-Africa Research Initiative (SAIS-CARI). Most of these funds, according to the China-Africa Research Initiative, are spent on addressing Africa's infrastructure gap with about 40 percent for power projects, and another 30 percent on modernizing transport infrastructure in the region.

Findings also show that the loans, which are given at comparatively low interest rates and with long repayment periods (a unique characteristic of Chinese loans to Africa), are also for investments in other areas, from oil and mining to manufacturing, telecommunications and agricultural sectors.

Although China's presence is more entrenched in Somalia and Uganda, there is a substantial presence in other sub-Saharan countries like Sudan, South Sudan, Kenya, Angola, Tanzania, Democratic Republic of Congo, Ethiopia, South Africa and Nigeria, where China has been involved in energy, mining and telecommunications, while also financing construction of roads, ports, airports, railways, schools, stadiums as well as funding cash crops plantations.

In 2015, for instance, China announced a $60 billion loans assistance to Africa for development, with President Xi Jinping of the Peoples Republic of China, saying, "The package would include zero-interest loans, as well as scholarships and training for thousands of Africans." The Chinese leader, who made the announcement at the 2015 investment summit between China and Africa in Johannesburg, the South African capital, told more than 35 African heads of state present at the occasion, that the momentum of rapid growth in African is "unstoppable."

The momentum of Chinese investment in Africa, has indeed been unstoppable, and it precedes Xi. Records show that trade volumes have been on a crescendo, from a meager $1 billion in 1980 to $5 billion in 1999, $10 billion in year 2000 and spiked to $39.7 billion in 2005. In 2006, the figure jumped to

$55 billion, and rose to $114 billion by 2010. By the next year 2011, it hit $166.3 billion and in the first ten months of 2012 it was already $163.9 billion.

At the same Forum on China-Africa Cooperation (FOCAC) in September 2018 in Beijing, President Xi pledged another $60 billion to Africa in loans, grants, and development financing. Xi also announced eight initiatives aimed at improving Sino-Africa relations, including investments in healthcare, education, security, cultural exchanges, and increasing non-resource imports from Africa.

Some analysts say there are as many as 800 Chinese companies in Africa, but a rather surprising McKinsey report from June 2017 estimated that, based on extensive fieldwork, there are more than 10,000 Chinese-owned firms operating in Africa, nearly four times the number from the Chinese Ministry of Commerce, according to Feyi Fawehinmi in Commentary magazine.

Fawehinmi argued that "no one can say for sure—not even the Chinese government—how many Chinese businesses are in Africa, never mind what they are doing there." This is partly because the businesses have mostly been careful to remain outside the spotlight and rarely ever speak to local media.

What is the Motivation?

This is a topical question that economic and development experts would really want answered, going by the unparalleled large number of Chinese businesses in virtually every country in the entire sub-Saharan Africa. Analysts say the Chinese are not just all over the region, but they curiously deepen their way into often seemingly impossible areas and circumstances and, surprisingly, are recording great successes.

An economic expert, Edward Miguel, in his book, *Africa's Turn*, relates that in his discussion with Chinese investors, it seems the key motive is simple - profit. In an environment where Europeans and US investors have largely shied away, Miguel states that "Africa provides bountiful profit opportunities across multiple economic sectors for Chinese firms flush with cash from their boundless growth at home."

Chinese investors also have a major advantage over their western counterparts in that they know how to make money in a developing country's business environment, where the rule of law is somewhat optional, corruption and bribery are the norm, and infrastructure is patchy. Their experiences at home give them a big leg up on the competition, Miguel added.

Others point out that China's venture into Africa is to meet its growing need for resources. Writing for the Council on Foreign Relations, a foreign policy powerhouse in Washington D.C., Eleanor Albert stated that China was focused on securing the long-term energy supplies needed to sustain its industrialization, searching for secure access to oil supplies and other raw materials around the globe and found them in abundance in Africa.

In corroborating Eleanor, it is on record that China's economy requires a substantial level of energy to run, and various countries in sub-Saharan Africa have that, a reason majority of the region's exports to China are comprised of mineral fuels, lubricants and related materials.

Besides the abundance of natural resources, China also finds sub-Saharan Africa a good investment destination because of the abundance of relatively cheap labor supply. Pervasive unemployment levels in this region and the ability of a Chinese firm to site an industry would make the African go for the job, not minding the size of the take home pay, thus affirming the popular adage that half a loaf is better than none.

It can therefore be surmised that widespread cheap labor in sub-Saharan countries, occasioned by the perennial high unemployment level, is a veritable attraction for the Chinese to these countries. This is more so as labor costs continue to rise in China.

Be that as it may, there is also the fact that if the local communities are hostile, the Chinese businessmen cannot settle in, much less investing. So, the receptivity of the local communities to the Chinese is also a good motivation, because no business can survive in a hostile environment.

There have, no doubt, been reported skirmishes between Chinese managers and local workers, but none has led to mass exodus of Chinese businesses, which shows that they indeed have a conducive business environment as part of the motivation.

What Do Africans Say?

It is common knowledge that the growing Chinese investment in sub-Saharan Africa span virtually every sector, from small food enterprises to massive technological and infrastructural projects. Although this has drawn sharp criticisms, especially from the United States, many Africans see grounds for optimism.

A recent CNN investigation into extensive Chinese investment in sub-Saharan Africa indicated that "turns out, they love them."

The CNN report cited Afrobarometer (a pan-

African series of national public attitude surveys on democracy, governance and society), which showed that almost two thirds or 63 percent of Africans say China's influence is somewhat positive, while only 15 per cent see it as somewhat or very negative.

"There is a negative narrative of China in Africa," says Anyway Chingwete, co-author of the study and project manager at Afrobarometer and the Institute for Justice and Reconciliation in Cape Town, South Africa, "but I believe ordinary citizens have a positive sentiment because of the contribution China has made to Africa."

The attitudes vary from country to country, with people in Mali (92 percent) Niger (84 percent) and Liberia (81 percent) being particularly glad to have them around. "This shows that African citizens are welcoming China's involvement," Chingwete said about his survey findings.

The report adds that it appears that it is not the Chinese culture that attracts Africans, but the potential for financial investment that China brings. Africans also like the Chinese for bringing affordable items like cars and mobile phones to the continent, says author, Mogopodi Lekorwe, a professor of Politics at the University of Botswana. "They used to be very expensive, but because these are now flooding the market, the prices have dropped."

Besides the perception of the generality of the people towards China, Abdi Latif Dahir, writing on this in Quartz Africa, described the disposition of many sub-Saharan Africa leaders towards China as "satisfied and inspired," as they all praise their alliance with China. The greatest indication of African leaders' support for Chinese investment in their countries was displayed when they spoke at the September 2018 meeting of FOCAC at Beijing.

At the forum, which had about 50 African Presidents in attendance, they all took turns to heap praises on President Xi and strongly defended China's deepening relationship with Africa, according to reports. President Paul Kagame of Rwanda, in his speech at the forum, described China-Africa relationship as "deeply transformational." Said he: "Africa is not a zero-sum game. Our growing ties with China do not come at anyone's expense. Indeed, the gains are enjoyed by everyone who does business on our continent." Kagame, who was then the rotating Chair of the African Union, and a critic of foreign aid, is reported to have praised Beijing's win-win-partnership.

South African President, Cyril Ramaphosa, co-chair of the forum, refuted criticism of colonialism in China-Africa relations and stated that "in the values that it promotes, in the manner that it operates and, in the impact that it has on African countries,

FOCAC refutes the view that a new colonialism is taking hold in Africa, as our detractors would have us believe."

Dahir reported that the Chinese used the forum to flaunt Kenya's $3.2 billion standard gauge railway as an example of how its infrastructural projects were changing the face of Africa. Many Kenyan officials at the forum were said to be busy signing billion-dollar deals with various Chinese investors; a development which prompted President Uhuru Kenyatta of Kenya to appreciate China's support of the country's development agenda, adding, "We are satisfied with the tremendous progress achieved in our bilateral cooperation."

Dahir further reported that, inspired by the impact China is making in his country, Ghanaian President, Nana Akufo-Addo said his country wants to duplicate China's success story. Ghana, he said, is "inspired by this model, and is trying to replicate same, I have urged others not to ignore Africa, and I am glad that China is, most certainly, not ignoring our continent." So also was the position of President Mokgweetsi Masisi of Botswana, who described the FOCAC forum as unique and encouraged China to keep up the innovation and friendliness with African countries.

Without having to go round all the countries in sub-Saharan Africa, and how they appreciate China's presence in their countries, one gets the impression that many leaders in the region overwhelmingly have a positive view of China's contributions to their countries and the visible improvements it has had in various sectors of the local economy.

This is not however, to say that everything is just fine with China's venture into the region. Fawehinmi captured this succinctly in an article in Quartz Africa, stating: "Even after many decades of doing business in Africa, Chinese businesses in Africa can hardly claim to be friends with their hosts." According to him, they operate "like ships that pass in the night and speak to each other in passing."

To Fawehinmi, the Chinese and their hosts continue to live side by side but far apart —the gap between them inevitably filled by mutual suspicion. He narrated that the Chinese in Lagos, for instance, retreat into their own world. In Nigeria, "I am yet to hear of a marriage between Chinese and Nigerians and it is hard to recall bumping into Chinese revelers on a night out or sharing a restaurant or bar with them," Fawehinmi disclosed.

The Criticisms

Without a doubt, China's growing business interest in Africa has faced criticisms from within and outside the sub-Saharan region. Both western and

African critics complain not just about what they refer to as China's controversial business model, but also about the country's alleged failure to promote good governance and human rights wherever they operate.

Some that have pushed back against China's business interest in Africa list their grievances to range from poor compliance with safety and environmental standards to unfair business practices and violation of local laws. Eleanor Albert wrote on Council on Foreign Relations website that the impression that China has exploited resources without building up local economies has triggered fierce criticism from even some African leaders.

According to Albert, in 2011, for example, Michael Sata won Zambia's presidency, in part by tapping into anti-Chinese sentiment, after Chinese managers shot protesters at a large coal mine in southern Zambia. He also alluded to the statement of Sanusi Lamido, former governor of Nigeria's Central Bank when he wrote in 2013 that "we must see China for what it is: a competitor, and Africa must recognize that China—like the United States, Russia, Britain, Brazil and the rest – are in Africa not for Africa's interests, but its own."

Findings show that some analysts in sub-Saharan Africa, especially civil society groups and labor union leaders have severally faulted Chinese companies for unfair labor practices, poor wages and working conditions. Others point at environmental concerns, while good governance watchdogs' frown at Chinese deals that take undue advantage of some African governments' relative weaknesses to foster corruption.

Researchers, Larry Hanauer and Lyle Morris, from their findings, say that in the view of some Africans, "China perpetuates a neo-colonial relationship in which Africa exports raw materials to China in exchange for manufactured goods." They reported that in some countries, resentment at Chinese business practices have led to popular protests and violence against Chinese businessmen.

The United States Perspective

There has not been a more vocal critic of Chinese investments in Africa than the United States. The United States government has not missed any opportunity over the years to indicate that China is pushing an unfair investment strategy in Africa; that the Chinese is exploiting African natural resources than spurring development in the region.

Virtually every successive administration in the United States, and indeed all American businesses, see China as a major threat to US interests in sub-

Saharan Africa. For instance, former US Secretary of State, Hillary Clinton in 2012 started an 11-day, seven-nation tour of Africa by contrasting America's commitment to democracy and human rights with China's focus on exploiting African resources. At her first stop in Senegal, the US Secretary of State, according to media reports, told a university audience that the US was committed to a model of sustainable partnership that added value, rather than extracted it from Africa, adding that unlike other countries, America would stand up for democracy and universal human rights even when it might be easier to look the other way and keep the resources flowing. She was apparently making a veiled comment of China's business interest in Africa.

But Emilio Viano, a professor at the American University who was part of the Secretary of State's entourage was not so vague, he told the Voice of America (VOA) that "one of the objectives of the visit is to compete with China and try to limit China's influence, business making and political power in Africa. The US wants to use this visit as a maneuver to limit the influence of China. This will not be done openly; it will be done, of course, diplomatically, without naming names, but certainly cautioning African leaders not to strike deals too easily with China."

However, whatever innuendos that might have been used hitherto to describe US perspective of China in Africa have been swept aside by the Trump administration. The Trump administration now brings American sentiment to the forefront by hinging the administration's African policy on activities of China in the region.

Shortly before his first and only visit to Africa, Trump's first Secretary of State (he has had so many in just three years), Rex Tillerson, accused China of using predatory loan practices, which he said, undermined growth and creating few, if any jobs in the sub-Saharan Africa. Addressing the African Union in Addis Ababa, Ethiopia, Tillerson charged the Chinese with providing opaque project loans that increased debt without providing significant training for the locals.

In announcing the US policy on Africa on December 13, 2018 at the Heritage Foundation, almost two years after assuming power, John Bolton, then US National Security Adviser, attacked Beijing for its "predatory" practices in Africa and asked African leaders to make a choice of whom to deal with. "China uses bribes, opaque agreements, and the strategic use of debt to hold states in Africa captive to Beijing's wishes and demands. Its investment ventures are riddled with corruption, and do not meet the same environmental or ethical standards as US developmental programs", Bolton, who was eventually out of the administration, stated in his speech.

Such predatory actions, he added, "are sub-components of broader Chinese strategic initiatives, including "One Belt, One Road" a plan to develop a series of trade routes leading to and from China with the ultimate goal of advancing Chinese global dominance." Pointing at the dysfunctional aspects of China in Zambia, Djibouti, the former US National Security Adviser added that between 1995 and 2006, US aid to Africa was roughly equal to the amount of assistance provided by all other donors combined, but regretted that "unfortunately, billions upon billions of US taxpayers' dollars have not achieved the desired effects."

According to him, "they have not stopped the scourge of terrorism, radicalism and violence; they have not prevented other powers, such as China and Russia from taking advantage of African states to increase their own power and influence; neither have they led to stable and transparent governance, economic viability and increasing development across the region."

Consequently, Bolton stated that the Trump African policy "will insist that US money is put to good use, and dollars sent to Africa are used efficiently to advance peace, stability, independence and prosperity for the region." In this direction, he disclosed that a new initiative called "Prosper Africa" would be developed to support US investments across the African continent.

The former National Security Adviser therefore "encouraged African leaders to choose high quality, transparent, inclusive and sustainable foreign investment projects, including those of United States," because, as he put it, "America's vision for the region is one of independence, self-reliance and growth—and not dependency, dominance and debt."

Under the new US-Africa policy, Bolton said US foreign aid, in every corner of the globe, would advance US interests and "countries that repeatedly vote against the United States in international forums, or take action counter to US interests, should not receive generous American foreign aid."

Analysis of global reaction to the Trump administration's policy on Africa, show that most diplomatic experts, while welcoming an exclusive US policy for Africa, frown at the details of the "New African strategy." Cornelia Tremann, a West African based analyst focused on China-Africa policy commented that "unfortunately, the positive aspects of the strategy were a little lost in the speech because the new US-Africa strategy is not really about Africa; it's about China."

Tremann, who runs an independent Africa and China focused advisory firm that assists governments and international organizations, added that "the policy is also too little too late, and asking countries to choose between the US or China is a bad idea and could backfire."

Writing in *Foreign Policy*, a publication of the US Council on Foreign Relations, Grant Harris made a bold projection that Trump's African policy is destined for failure. Corroborating Tremann, Harris stated that "at its heart, the strategy is about countering China. The administration is right to worry about Beijing's aggressive diplomacy in Africa, and Bolton's speech provided a welcome vision after two years of listless US policy toward the continent. But the new strategy misses the mark. While the Trump administration focuses on the commercial threat from China, Beijing is investing in long-term relationships, not just trade and infrastructure. The United States needs to offer African countries a compelling alternative if it is to counter China."

Former President of Nigeria, Olusegun Obasanjo, and Greg Mills, chairman, Brenthrust Foundation, also raised some concerns on the new US-Africa strategy. "China's relationship with the continent is not all bad, far from it. Nor can we say that the US relationship with the continent is universally beneficial to all recipients", they wrote.

Writing in *Quartz Africa*, Obasanjo and Mills maintained that China's second coming in Africa, the first being a short-lived intervention during the wars of liberation in the 1960s and 1970s, has transformed the image of the continent from largely one of a problem to be solved to a commercial prospect.

Commenting on the call to African leaders to choose between US and China, they noted that "while there is nothing wrong with greater competition over ideas, Africa is likely to resist making a choice between China and the United States. The US is asking African countries to choose sides at a time when many don't have this luxury."

Given that the US has always expressed discomfort on China's aggressive investments in sub-Saharan Africa, the US position is not helped by such aggressive posture. When combined with Trump's "America first" mantra, the New Africa Strategy becomes counterproductive. This is because a policy that requires an entire region to choose between US and China reminds one of the Cold War days, when leaders in Africa needed to align themselves with either the US or communist countries. Like most of the Trump administration policies, it sure looks archaic.

Many diplomatic experts on Africa criticize the new US African policy for lack of substance. They say it is not only haughty, but also reveals a total lack of willingness by the United States to engage, but rather control and dominate. But there are still some in the US who think that the situation could be handled better; who are of the opinion that the two superpowers should find a way of working together, without replaying the sordid history of superpower rivalry in Africa and its attendant negative outcomes.

One of those championing this approach is former US President, Jimmy Carter. The former president warns the United States against the risk of sliding into a commerce war with China, calling on the two countries to find a common ground on Africa development. Carter made the call while marking the 40th anniversary of his January 1979 normalization of relations with Chinese leader, Deng Xiaoping. Frowning at the current situation where both countries are increasingly seeing the other as a threat, the former US president said, "If top government officials embrace these dangerous notions, a modern cold war is not inconceivable."

According to Carter, "At this sensitive moment, misconceptions, miscalculations and failure to follow carefully defined rules of engagement in areas, such as the Taiwan Strait and South China Sea, could escalate into military conflict, creating a worldwide catastrophe."

As a moderating voice to Trump's characteristic bellicose approach, President Carter said, "Africa, like billions of other people around the world do not want to be forced to choose a side. By working together with Africans, the United States and China would also be helping themselves overcome distrust and rebuild this vital relationship."

Acceptance versus Antagonism

But the question remains, why is there very strong support of China ventures in Africa on the one hand, and an equally very strong antagonism of China in Africa, on the other hand? In attempting to answer this poser, one notes that while the relics of the Cold War and perhaps neocolonialistic tendencies are not to be ignored, it is also expedient to ascertain the true picture of China's investment in Africa with a dispassionate mindset.

It is in search of this apolitical assessment that the research work by Deborah Brautigam is worth considering. Brautigam is the Bernard L. Schwartz professor of International Political Economy and director of China Africa Research Initiative at John

Hopkins School of Advanced International Studies. In a research report published in the April 12, 2018 edition of *The World Post*, a collaborative pull-out between Berggruen Institute and the Washington Post newspaper, she stated that "researchers who have explored China's role in Africa suggest that many of the things our politicians believe about Chinese engagement are not actually true."

Brautigam, in the publication, presented a summary of findings from various researchers and the academia, including the ones she and others carried out at the China Africa Research Initiative at John Hopkins School of Advanced International Studies. The article is reproduced here unedited in the interest of the reading public.

1. *Jobs and training*:

Lina Benabdallah, a political science professor at Wake Forest University, studies Chinese investments in African human resource development programs. "Africans are being invited to Chinese universities. China is offering scholarships," she said. "When Africans are thinking about technology [and] skills, they are thinking of China as a valid option."

Surveys of employment on Chinese projects in Africa repeatedly find that three-quarters or more of the workers are, in fact, local. This makes business sense.

In China, textile workers now earn about $500 a month — far more than workers in most African countries. Chinese investors flocking to set up factories in low-cost countries like Ethiopia are not thinking about importing Chinese workers. Like U.S. and European factory owners who moved their factories to China in past decades, Chinese firms are now outsourcing their own manufacturing to cheaper countries.

2. Predatory lending:

Are the Chinese engaging in predatory lending? Here, researchers can also shine light on a murky subject. Scholars at Boston University and Johns Hopkins University have been painstakingly assembling databases of Chinese loans provided since 2000.

In Africa, we found that China had lent at least $95.5 billion between 2000 and 2015. That's a lot of debt. Yet by and large, the Chinese loans in our database were performing a useful service: financing Africa's serious infrastructure gap. On a continent where over 600 million Africans have no access to electricity, 40 percent of the Chinese loans paid for power generation and transmission. Another 30 percent went to modernizing Africa's crumbling transport infrastructure.

Some of these were no doubt pork barrel projects and white elephants: airports with few passengers, or bridges to nowhere. African presidents, like others, love to cut ribbons and leave legacies of big buildings. Chinese companies will receive nearly all of the contracts to build this Chinese-financed infrastructure. Questions have been raised about its quality. Yet on the whole, power and transport are investments that boost economic growth. And we found that Chinese loans generally have comparatively low interest rates and long repayment periods.

3. Land grabs:

"Land grabs" — a term used for any purchase, rental or theft of relatively large amounts of land — are controversial around the world, but especially in Africa, where colonial powers like Britain and France grabbed nearly the entire continent. The stories that China was now a "land grabber" in Africa seemed to make sense. After all, China has 9 percent of the world's arable land, 6 percent of its water and over 20 percent of its people. Africa has plentiful land and the planet's largest expanses of underutilized land and water. And Chinese companies were clearly interested in investing in Africa; some came to inquire about land.

And so the land grab rumors began to spread. On the CBS News website, we read: "China recently purchased half the farmland under cultivation in the Congo." German Chancellor Angela Merkel's top African adviser told reporters that a devastating famine in the Horn of Africa several years ago was partly due to China's "large-scale land purchases." Even Swedish crime writer Henning Mankell recirculated a "land grab" story: "I read just the other day that China has rented land in Kenya to move some one million peasants to Africa."

Intrigued by these stories, I did what academics do. Instead of tweeting what might have been fake news, I set up a research project.

Our team at the International Food Policy Research Institute and at Johns Hopkins University collected a database of 57 cases where Chinese firms (or the government) were alleged to have acquired or negotiated large (over 500 hectare) amounts of African farmland. If all of these media reports had been real news, this would have amounted to a very alarming 6 million hectares — 1 percent of all the farmland in Africa.

We spent three years tracking down every single case. We travelled from Madagascar to Mozambique, Zimbabwe to Zambia. We confirmed that nearly a third of these stories, including the three above, were literally false. In the remaining cases, we found real Chinese investments. But the total amount of land actually acquired by Chinese firms was only about 240,000 hectares: 4 percent of the reported amount.

The stories of large-scale land grabbing and Chinese peasants being shipped to Africa to grow food for China turned out to be mostly myths. As researchers at the

Center for International Forestry Research concluded after their own rigorous research: "China is not a dominant investor in plantation agriculture in Africa, in contrast to how it is often portrayed."

We found a story of globalization, not colonization; a story of African agency, rather than Chinese rapacity. In Mozambique, I met African investors like Zaidi Aly, who had traveled to Brazil to learn how to grow soybeans for local chicken feed. There, he met a Chinese firm buying soybeans. Aly invited them to invest in soybeans with him. Hit by a prolonged drought, their joint venture failed. The Chinese returned home. But Aly told me it was a net gain: "I learned so much from them."

To be sure, increased Chinese engagement comes with significant and very real challenges for many Africans. Traders complain about competition from Chinese migrants. In our research on Chinese factories in Africa, we've interviewed African workers who now have jobs but complain about Chinese bosses who expect long hours at low pay.

Chinese demand for African ivory, abalone, rhinoceros' tusk and materials from other endangered species has taken a significant toll on conservation efforts. And Chinese President Xi Jinping's recent lifting of his own term limits is bound to embolden African leaders who are reluctant to leave their comfortable presidential posts.

111

China is often lambasted as a nefarious actor in its African dealings, but the evidence tells a more complicated story. Chinese loans are powering Africa, and Chinese firms are creating jobs. China's agricultural investment is far more modest than reported and welcomed by some Africans. China may boost Africa's economic transformation, or they may get it wrong — just as American development efforts often go awry.

CHAPTER SEVEN

What Do Africans Stand to Lose?

D onald Trump prides himself in always having the last say in any argument. As belittling and unstatesmanlike as that may be, it does not bother him.

Whenever he is at the losing end of an argument, with his notoriously inferior polemics, he will typically throw in the towel with his handy contumelious question, "What do you have to lose?"

He recently displayed this atrocious trait during his abysmal management of the coronavirus pandemic when, against the advice of medical experts, he wanted the use of untested hydroxychloroquine in treating those infected with the virus. When he realized he could not lord it over the medical professionals, he said, "What do you have to lose [in using the medication]?"

That was not the first time Trump was using his favorite, brash rhetorical question. It was initially used during the 2016 presidential election, when he could not have a headway with African American voters.

On Thursday, August 18, 2016, in North Carolina, he asked them, again and again, "What do you stand to lose voting for me?" The chant became his battle cry. Jenna Johnson reported then in the Washington Post that Trump "repeated it at a rally in Michigan on Friday evening and Virginia on Saturday night. In Ohio on Monday, Trump expanded his pitch to include Hispanics."

From then till the end of the campaign, the chant became a rallying cry for Trump at every campaign stop and often went as reported here by the Washington Post:

> *"Our government has totally failed our African American friends, our Hispanic friends and the people of our country. Period," Trump said in Akron, Ohio, straying from the prepared remarks the campaign provided to reporters. "The Democrats have failed completely in the inner cities. For those hurting the most who have been failed and failed by their politician — year after year, failure after failure, worse numbers after worse numbers. Poverty. Rejection. Horrible education. No housing, no homes, no ownership. Crime at levels*

that nobody has seen. You can go to war zones in countries that we are fighting and it's safer than living in some of our inner cities that are run by the Democrats. And I ask you this, I ask you this — crime, all of the problems — to the African Americans, who I employ so many, so many people, to the Hispanics, tremendous people: What the hell do you have to lose? Give me a chance. I'll straighten it out. I'll straighten it out. What do you have to lose?" The mostly white crowd would cheer and then started chanting: "Trump! Trump! Trump! Trump!"

Trump would continue: "And you know, I say it, and I'm going to keep saying it. And some people say: 'Wow, that makes sense.' And then some people say: 'Well, that wasn't very nice.' Look, it is a disaster the way African Americans are living, in many cases, and, in many cases the way Hispanics are living, and I say it with such a deep-felt feeling: What do you have to lose? I will straighten it out. I'll bring jobs back. We'll bring spirit back. We'll get rid of the crime. You'll be able to walk down the street without getting shot. Right now, you walk down the street, you get shot. Look at the statistics. We'll straighten it out. If you keep voting for the same failed politicians, you will keep getting the same results. They don't care about you. They just like you once every four years — get your vote and then they say: 'Bye, bye!'"

The campaign rhetoric did not go down well with his

opponent, the Hilary Clinton campaign, with Clinton's director of state campaigns and political engagement, Marlon Marshall saying then that Trump is "doubling down on his insults, fear and stereotypes that set our community back and further divide our country. But again, this is not surprising, this is a man who questions the citizenship of the first African American president, has a disturbing pattern of courting white supremacists, and has been sued for housing discrimination against communities of color."

Condemnation of that rhetoric was not only from Hillary Clinton campaign, a host of others expressed surprise at such campaign style. The BBC reported that some observers called it an act of desperation.

Some analysts say Mr. Trump, trailing badly in national polls for weeks, desperately needs to broaden his appeal beyond his base of white working-class voters, the BBC reported, adding that others were just 'perplexed.'

"This is Trump's SALES PITCH to black voters, ostensibly. Telling us we're dumb, broke suckers who have no jobs is the best he could do," Jamil Smith, a black reporter for MTV News, wrote on Twitter.

Ana Navarro, a Latina Republican strategist, wrote: "Trump's 'Black outreach' so tone-deaf and condescending, his 'Hispanic outreach', (eating a taco bowl), suddenly not that bad and stupid."

Ominous Signal

Keen followers of the Trump presidency say Trump may, for all we know, be using same method in relating with sub-Saharan Africa. The reasoning is that if Trump has such a low perception of African-Americans, it goes without saying that he is not likely to have a better impression of black African countries and their people.

A sign of this demeaning and retreating posture manifested very early in his presidency. The administration initiated a rocky relationship with Africa as Trump cut aid to the continent by as much as 35 per cent in his very first budget proposals. Announcing the proposals, the administration put it this way, *"The President's $5.2 billion FY 2018 foreign assistance request for Africa reflects the Administration's focus on economic and development assistance to countries of the greatest strategic importance to the United States, such as those critical to advancing U.S. national security objectives...[We] had to make some difficult tradeoffs."*

This figure was down from $8 billion in 2015 and signaled, in effect, that President Trump would engage in selective assistance to only countries "of the greatest strategic importance to the US", to the detriment of the rest of the region. David Himbara, Toronto-based professor of International Development, observed that "assistance to the needy has no place in the new administration."

With the outcome of the 2016 presidential election, Trump was indeed given a chance as he campaigned, but more than three years into his presidency, the report card *vis-a-vis* his impact on black Africa tells a very uncomfortable story. The African continent and African Americans have not fared better. In particular, the answer to his question, "What do you stand to lose?" is very apparent. Trump has substantially cut aid to Africa-This is the first thing the sub-Saharan region, black Africa, has lost in the Trump presidency - *no more assistance to those in need.*

Deeper Implications

A larger ramification of the budget cuts was expounded by a Reuters investigative report in May 2018 by Tim Cocks. The report has it that "to please Christian conservatives who strongly oppose abortion and are a major part of Trump's political base," the president approved a cut of all funding from USAID grant to the Marie Stopes Ladies (MSL), as part of a ban on funding to any foreign Nongovernment Organization (NGO) offering advice on abortion anywhere. The MS Ladies drive from village to village in the remote part of Burkina Faso offering free contraception, advice on family planning, sexual health and sometimes post-abortion care.

According to the report, the NGO said the contraceptive program is crucial in Burkina Faso, where the fertility rate is 5.5 births per woman. In some villages, the report stated, the MS Ladies operate from government centers, supplementing the limited services on offer as well as paying for training of health workers in many government clinics. MSL lamented that the cuts would negatively affect thousands of people in Burkina Faso and that it had been forced to axe 22 out of 62 outreach teams of voucher programs in Madagascar.

Also, consequent upon the cut, 17 out of 35 programs in Uganda are gone, and in Zimbabwe, where MSL has an extensive presence, it cut down half of the 1200 teams it had from village to village.

The Reuters report added that in the same vein, the International Planned Parenthood Federation, IPPF had cut 22 programs in sub-Saharan Africa and had others closing in Togo, Ethiopia and Ivory Coast, mainly because it lost USAID funding, according to Caroline Kwamboka, IPPF's senior advocacy manager for Africa.

MSL and the International Planned Parenthood Federation offer abortion services, in accordance with local rules, and say it is a last resort in preventing unwanted or unsafe births. The direct impact of the funding *cut squeezes family planning services in the region* - another thing Africans lost with the Trump presidency.

Over three years into his presidency, close watchers of US-Africa affairs say Trump has shown little interest in Africa and has made minimal engagement with leaders from black Africa. The little attempt Trump made on sidelines of the 2017 United Nations General Assembly turned out awkward and remembered more for the snide comments referenced earlier in this book, than for anything worthwhile. This is yet another thing Africans stand to lose with the Trump presidency - *lack of meaningful engagement.*

No one explains US-Africa relations better than career diplomat and former US Ambassador to Nigeria, John Campbell. In his piece in the November 3, 2017 edition of Foreign Policy magazine titled, "Trump's Dangerous Retreat from Africa", the former ambassador stated that Trump's disinterest in Africa appears to be shared by many in his cabinet, including former Secretary of State, Rex Tillerson, who at an hour-long meeting with State Department employees on August 1, 2017, embarked on a "little walk ... around the world" that did not mention Africa and its 1.2 billion inhabitants — roughly 17 percent of the world's population.

"As one might expect, given his disinterest in Africa — though with the caveat that his administration is less than a year — Trump has unveiled no signature initiative there that could be compared to Barack Obama's Power Africa plan, which aimed to harness public and private funds to increase electricity generation, or to George W. Bush's widely successful President's Emergency Plan for Aids Relief (PEPFAR)," Campbell wrote.

According to the former US ambassador to Nigeria, while the administration's 2018 budget proposal explicitly stated that it would be "continuing treatment for all current HIV/AIDS patients" under PEPFAR (which provided life-saving antiretroviral drugs to 11.5 million people last year), in reality, the proposal would instead lower the yearly contribution by 17 percent, or about $800 million.

Very little or nothing is known about the future of Power Africa, Obama's pivotal power generation project which delivered electricity to more than 50 million people since 2013. There is however not much hope here since the Trump administration has already shown itself to be hostile to most of the Obama administration's initiatives. Not a good omen for the power project; and there goes another loss to the region—*the stalling or discontinuation of the much vaunted power project.*

It is imperative to mention that in early October 2018, President Trump signed $60 billion foreign aid for companies willing to do business in developing countries in Africa, Asia and the Americas, barely one month after China President Xi gave out $60 billion at the annual FOCAC meeting in Beijing to African Countries.

The US foreign aid in loans, loan guarantees and insurance to be managed by United States International Development Finance Corporation (USIDC) could be said to have been an afterthought for the US president who had vehemently criticized foreign aid from when he announced his bid for presidency. This is in addition to his recommended deep cuts to foreign aid in his first budget proposals as President.

Glenn Thrush, writing for the New York Times gave a good explanation: "The President's shift has less to do with a sudden embrace of foreign aid than a desire to block Beijing's plan for economic, technological and political dominance. China has spent nearly five years bankrolling a plan to gain greater global influence by financing big projects across Asia, Eastern Europe and Africa."

This underscores the definitive motivation for Trump to have anything to do in Africa-obstructing China. It is devoid of any genuine compassion to help those in the region, as with President George W. Bush or Bill Clinton. This is not in any way a gain for Africa, if anything, the *Africans are losing out* because, with Trump, Africa is like a *pawn in the chess game, to be manipulated and sacrificed.*

As reported by Thrush, "The bigger question is whether it will do anything to reduce China's global influence," especially in sub-Saharan Africa. Nobody thinks so because Trump has already lost the fight for Africa with his *disparagement of the entire region.*

Not even African Americans are gaining from Trump's presidency. Besides various orchestrated plans by Trump backers to disenfranchise African American voters, an avalanche of news reports showed that in the height of the coronavirus pandemic, the virus was killing a disproportionate number of African Americans than any other group.

A brief analysis, as at April 10, 2020, from various news reports showed that 70 per cent of deaths were African Americans. In Milwaukee County, with 28 per cent of black population, 73 percent of deaths were African Americans. Louisiana has 32 per cent of blacks, but 70 percent of deaths were African Americans. Michigan has 14 percent of African Americans, but recorded 40 per cent of deaths to coronavirus, and the list went on.

Surgeon General of the United States, Jerome Adams, while commenting on this unfortunate scenario said, "They are getting hit hard." Major Lori Lightfoot, Major of Chicago City, described it as "devastating." Doctor Sanjay Gupta on CNN attributed the high death record of African Americans to a high rate of diabetes, hypertension and lack of access to healthcare and ongoing misinformation by some government officials led by the President, who when pressed at a media availability said he was "cheerleading," instead of showing leadership.

According to Gupta, the black folks are people that "find it hard to get needed tests, less likely to be tested and more likely to be on the frontlines as nurses, doctors and nursing assistants." This was corroborated by Lightfoot, who stated: "This is about healthcare accessibility, life expectancy, joblessness and hunger." Lightfoot added, "We're seeing this manifest in large urban areas with large black populations all over the United States. Milwaukee, Cleveland, Detroit ... are experiencing the same thing. But we are going to step up and do something about it."

That situation does not seem like that of people who have nothing to lose, they indeed have a lot to lose and are losing, big time, under the current regime. In his reaction, Trump said he was going to look at the statistics. *Recording the highest number of deaths in a pandemic* that could have been contained earlier with proactive federal response is again, what black African American brothers and sisters lost.

The Washington Post in a study published on January 17, 2020 surmised that, "Black Americans are deeply pessimistic about the country under Trump, whom more than 8 in 10 describe as "racist". Post-Ipsos finds.

The Washington Post newspaper reported that, "President Trump made a stark appeal to black Americans during the 2016 election when he asked, "What have you got to lose?" three years later, black Americans have rendered their verdict on his presidency with a deeply pessimistic assessment of their place in the United States under a leader seen by an overwhelming majority as racist."

In the Washington Post-Ipsos poll, many respondents spoke out their mind. In particular, respondents were asked to say how Trump's presidency had affected them personally or African Americans in general. "Donald Trump has not done anything for the African American people," said one person. "He has created an atmosphere of division and overt racism and fear of immigrants unseen in many years," said another. A third said, "He has taken hatred against people of color, in general, from the closet to the front porch." The report disclosed.

Taking the economy and unemployment, the president routinely talks about how a steadily growing economy and historically low unemployment have resulted in more African Americans with jobs recorded. Trumps says frequently that what he has done for African Americans in two-and -half years, no president has been able to do anything like it. However, everyone knows that Trump speaks in hyperboles that are very different from reality.

The Washington Post survey indicated that the facts do not support Trump's statement. This is because "a 77 percent majority of black Americans say Trump deserves 'only some' or 'hardly any' credit for the 5.5 per cent unemployment rate among black adults compared with 20 percent who said Trump deserves significant credit."

In follow-up interviews, according to the publication, many said former president Barack Obama deserves more credit for the improvement in the unemployment rate, which declined from a high of 16.8 per cent in 2010 to 7.5 percent when he left office.

The report added, "Black Americans report little change in their personal financial situations in the past few years, with 19 percent saying it has been getting better and 26 percent saying it has been getting worse. Most, 54 percent, say their financial situation has stayed the same."

The numerous things black Africans and their African Americans Kith and Kin stand to lose from the Trump presidency are best surmised from his current Africa Strategy launched in December 2018, about two years into his presidency. The policy paper as reproduced in this book unedited is a clear roadmap that aptly articulates Trump's apparent disinterest, and what analysts describe as an unprecedented awkward disposition to black Africa by a sitting US President.

The policy paper does not give any indication of the willingness to engage or be involved, but rather threaten and antagonize. Ambassador Campbell nailed Trump administration's lack of propensity to negotiate, as he highlighted the paucity of staff on the African desk at the State Department. Campbell noted here that "important African diplomatic posts remain unfilled, and domestic positions concerned with Africa have been filled only very slowly. For his meetings with African heads of state on the margins of the U.N. General Assembly, career State and Defense officials were not invited to be present."

The sad implication of this sordid state of affairs is that the African region, as it is, *does not have diplomats advocating for it at the table*. This, too, is another loss to the region.

Remarks by National Security Advisor Ambassador John R. Bolton on the Trump Administration's New Africa Strategy

Issued on: December 13, 2018
As delivered on December 13, 2018.
Heritage Foundation, Washington, D.C.

Well, Kim, thanks very much, and thanks to you and Kay for inviting me here. I'm delighted again to be here at the Heritage, an institution that really has contributed so much to the public policy debate for many decades now in the United States. And I'm particularly pleased to be here to unveil the Trump administration's new Africa Strategy, which the President approved yesterday, and which the administration will begin executing immediately.

This strategy is the result of an intensive interagency process, and reflects the core tenets of President Trump's foreign policy doctrine. Importantly, the strategy remains true to his central campaign promise to put the interests of the American People first, both at home and abroad.

The White House is proud to finalize this strategy during the second year of President Trump's first term, about two years earlier than the prior administration's release of its Africa strategy.

We have prioritized developing this document because we understand that lasting stability, prosperity, independence, and security on the African continent are in the national security interest of the United States.

Under our new approach, every decision we make, every policy we pursue, and every dollar of aid we spend will further U.S. priorities in the region. In particular, the strategy addresses three core U.S. interests on the continent:

First, advancing U.S. trade and commercial ties with nations across the region to the benefit of both the United States and Africa.

We want our economic partners in the region to thrive, prosper, and control their own destinies. In America's economic dealings, we ask only for reciprocity, never for subservience.

Second, countering the threat from Radical Islamic Terrorism and violent conflict.

ISIS, al-Qaida, and their affiliates all operate and recruit on the African continent, plotting attacks against American citizens and targets. Any sound U.S. strategy toward Africa must address this serious threat in a comprehensive way.

And third, we will ensure that U.S. taxpayer dollars for aid are used efficiently and effectively.

The United States will no longer provide indiscriminate assistance across the entire continent, without focus or prioritization. And, we will no longer support unproductive, unsuccessful, and unaccountable U.N. peacekeeping missions.

We want something more to show for Americans' hard-earned taxpayer dollars.

Under our new Africa strategy, we will target U.S. funding toward key countries and particular strategic objectives. All U.S. aid on the continent will advance U.S. interests, and help African nations move toward self-reliance.

Our first priority, enhancing U.S. economic ties with the region, is not only essential to improving opportunities for American workers and businesses; it is also vital to safeguarding the economic independence of African states and protecting U.S. national security interests.

Great power competitors, namely China and Russia, are rapidly expanding their financial and political influence across Africa. They are deliberately and aggressively targeting their investments in the region to gain a competitive advantage over the United States.

From 2016-2017, China's foreign direct investment toward Africa totaled $6.4 billion dollars. And, over the past several years, China has devoted considerable state-directed and state-supported financing to projects in the region.

China uses bribes, opaque agreements, and the strategic use of debt to hold states in Africa captive to Beijing's wishes and demands. Its investment ventures are riddled with corruption, and do not meet the same environmental or ethical standards as U.S. developmental programs.

Such predatory actions are sub-components of broader Chinese strategic initiatives, including "One Belt, One Road"—a plan to develop a series of trade routes leading to and from China with the ultimate goal of advancing Chinese global dominance.

In Africa, we are already seeing the disturbing effects of China's quest to obtain more political, economic, and military power.

The nation of Zambia, for example, is currently in debt to China to the tune of $6 to $10 billion dollars. China is now poised to take over Zambia's national power and utility company in order to collect on Zambia's financial obligations.

Similarly, from 2014 to 2016, Djibouti's external public debt-to-GDP ratio ballooned from fifty percent to eighty-five percent, with most of that debt owed to China.

In 2017, China established a military base in Djibouti that is only miles from our U.S. base, Camp Lemonnier, which supports critical U.S. operations to counter violent terrorist organizations in East Africa.

In May, U.S. officials accused China of using military-grade lasers from this base to target and distract U.S. pilots on ten different occasions. Two of our American pilots suffered eye injuries from exposure to laser beams.

And soon, Djibouti may hand over control of the Doraleh Container Terminal, a strategically-located shipping port on the Red Sea, to Chinese state-owned enterprises.

Should this occur, the balance of power in the Horn of Africa—astride major arteries of maritime trade between Europe, the Middle East, and South Asia— would shift in favor of China. And, our U.S. military personnel at Camp Lemonnier, could face even further challenges in their efforts to protect the American people.

Russia, for its part, is also seeking to increase its influence in the region through corrupt economic dealings. Across the continent, Russia advances its political and economic relationships with little regard for the rule of law or accountable and transparent governance.

It continues to sell arms and energy in exchange for votes at the United Nations—votes that keep strongmen in power, undermine peace and security, and run counter to the best interests of the African people.

Russia also continues to extract natural resources from the region for its own benefit.

In short, the predatory practices pursued by China and Russia stunt economic growth in Africa; threaten the financial independence of African nations; inhibit opportunities for U.S. investment; interfere with U.S. military operations; and pose a significant threat to U.S. national security interests.

Equally concerning at this time, the lack of economic progress in the region has accompanied the proliferation of Radical Islamic Terrorism, and other forms of violent conflict, across Africa.

Countering these serious threats is the second priority under our new Africa strategy.

In recent years, ISIS, al-Qaida, and other terrorists operating in Africa have increased the lethality of their attacks, expanded into new areas, and repeatedly targeted U.S. citizens and interests.

In Mali, JNIM, Jama'at Nusrat al-Islam wal-Muslimin—which describes itself as an al-Qaida affiliate—is increasing in strength and has killed and wounded scores of peacekeepers, partner forces, and innocent civilians, in addition to kidnapping Westerners and threatening U.S. allies.

In Libya, the local ISIS-affiliate has found fertile ground to recruit new terrorists and plot attacks against the United States.

In South Sudan, an ongoing civil war has ravaged a young nation, displaced millions, and led to the deaths of hundreds of thousands of people.

The continuing threat from terrorism and other violent conflicts across the region puts American lives at risk, and drains vital American resources.

Between 2014 and 2018, the United States provided approximately $3.76 billion dollars in humanitarian aid to South Sudan and refugees in neighboring countries.

This number represents only a small amount of the total aid that the United States devotes to Africa.

In fact, in Fiscal Year 2017, the Department of State and USAID provided approximately $8.7 billion dollars in development, security, and food assistance to Africa.

In Fiscal Year 2016, we provided approximately $8.3 billion dollars.

Between 1995 and 2006, U.S. aid to Africa was roughly equal to the amount of assistance provided by all other donors combined.

Unfortunately, billions upon billions of U.S. taxpayer dollars have not achieved the desired effects.

They have not stopped the scourge of terrorism, radicalism, and violence.

They have not prevented other powers, such as China and Russia, from taking advantage of African states to increase their own power and influence.

And, they have not led to stable and transparent governance, economic viability, and increasing development across the region.

From now on, the United States will not tolerate this longstanding pattern of aid without effect, assistance without accountability, and relief without reform.

Instead, we are pursuing a new path, one that, we hope, finally gets results.

Americans are a generous people, but we insist that our money is put to good use.

Our third priority, therefore, is ensuring that all U.S. assistance dollars sent to Africa are used efficiently and effectively to advance peace, stability, independence, and prosperity in the region.

Here are some of the specific, bold actions we will take under our new strategy to address the three priority areas I have just highlighted.

To expand our economic relationships in the region, we are developing a new initiative called "Prosper Africa," which will support U.S. investment across the continent, grow Africa's middle class, and improve the overall business climate in the region.

In addition, we will encourage African leaders to choose high-quality, transparent, inclusive, and sustainable foreign investment projects, including those from the United States. We will leverage our expanded and modernized development tools to support access to financing and provide strong alternatives to external state-directed initiatives.

America's vision for the region is one of independence, self-reliance, and growth—not dependency, domination, and debt.

We want African nations to succeed, flourish, and remain independent in fact and not just in theory.

In the coming years and months, we also intend to pursue modern, comprehensive trade agreements on the continent that ensure fair and reciprocal exchange between the United States and the nations of Africa. We will begin these negotiations on a bilateral basis, and focus on creating mutually beneficial partnerships.

Our new economic initiatives in Africa will help support American jobs and expand market access for U.S. exports, while promoting sustainable growth in African countries.

We will focus our economic efforts on African governments that act with us as strategic partners, and, which are striving toward improved governance and transparent business practices.

As our partner nations develop economically, they will be better prepared to address a range of security threats, including terrorism and militant violence.

Under our new strategy, we will also take several additional steps to help our African friends fight terrorism and strengthen the rule of law. We will assist key African governments in building the capacity of partner forces and security institutions to provide effective and sustainable security and law enforcement services to their citizens.

Our goal is for the nations of the region to take ownership over peace and security in their own neighborhood.

The G5 Sahel Joint Force, comprised of Mauritania, Niger, Chad, Burkina Faso, and Mali, which the United States supports, is a great example of the enormous potential for African joint security cooperation.

The G5 Sahel Joint Force is seeking to build regional capability to combat terrorism, transnational organized crime, and human trafficking in the Sahel.

As this force gains capacity, G5 countries must remain in the driver's seat—this initiative cannot be outsourced to the U.N. for funding and other support.

We want to see more cooperative regional security organizations like these emerge around the world.

As part of our new Africa strategy, the United States

will also reevaluate its support for U.N. peacekeeping missions. We will only back effective and efficient operations, that we will seek to streamline, reconfigure, or terminate missions that are unable to meet their own mandate or facilitate lasting peace. Our objective is to resolve conflicts, not freeze them in perpetuity.

And, we will not provide legitimacy to missions that give large payouts to countries sending poorly-equipped soldiers who provide insufficient protection to vulnerable populations on the ground.

The sexual exploitation and abuse by UN peacekeepers of the very populations that they were sent to protect has been, and remains, completely unacceptable. Continued malfeasance without consequences damages the integrity of the entire U.N. peacekeeping system. If we are truly committed to protecting innocent life in conflict zones, then we must insist on accountable, robust, and effective peacekeeping operations.

In April, the United States did just that regarding the decades-old U.N. peacekeeping mission in Western Sahara. We demanded a six month, rather than annual, renewal period for the mission, and we insisted on a stronger, more effective mandate tied to substantive political progress.

Because of our actions, the parties to the conflict and key neighboring countries agreed to meet for the first time since 2012. Last week, the U.N. Envoy hosted these talks in Geneva and the participants agreed to hold additional talks in early next year.

Moving forward, we will also ensure that bilateral U.S. security assistance targets nations that act as responsible regional stakeholders, and nations where state failure or weakness would pose a direct threat to the United States and our citizens. We want to use American dollars in the most efficient way to protect the interests of the American people.

Accordingly, we will make certain that ALL aid to the region—whether for security, humanitarian, or development needs—advances these U.S. interests.

Countries that receive U.S. assistance must invest in health and education, encourage accountable and transparent governance, support fiscal transparency, and promote the rule of law.

The administration will not allow hard-earned taxpayer dollars to fund corrupt autocrats, who use the money to fill their coffers at the expense of their people, or commit gross human rights abuses.

For example, the United States is now reviewing its assistance to South Sudan to ensure that our aid does not prolong the conflict or facilitate predatory behavior. We will not provide loans or more American resources to a South Sudanese government led by the same morally bankrupt leaders, who perpetuate the horrific violence and immense human suffering in South Sudan.

The administration is also developing a new foreign assistance strategy to improve the effectiveness of American foreign aid worldwide. American foreign assistance was originally designed to counter the Soviet Union during the Cold War, and most recently to fight terrorism after 9/11.

Today, we need to make adjustments to address the pressing challenge of great power competition, and to correct past mistakes in structuring our funding.

In developing our strategy, we are revisiting the foundational principles of the Marshall Plan. The Marshall Plan furthered American interests, bypassed the United Nations, and targeted key sectors of foreign economies rather than dissipating aid across hundreds of programs.

Our new foreign assistance strategy will ensure that all U.S. foreign aid, in every corner of the globe, advances U.S. interests.

Our goal is to move recipient states toward self-reliance, and prevent long-term dependency.

Structural reforms will likely be critical, including practicing fiscal responsibility, promoting fair and reciprocal trade, deregulating economies, and supporting the private sector.

We should emphasize bilateral mechanisms to maintain maximum American control over every American dollar spent.

Less needy recipients should graduate from foreign assistance, and assistance should decline to countries and organizations making poor policy choices.

In addition, we should target resources toward areas where we have the most impact to ensure efficient use of taxpayer dollars.

Countries that repeatedly vote against the United States in international forums, or take action counter to U.S. interests, should not receive generous American foreign aid.

The United States will respect the independence of other nations in providing humanitarian, security, and development assistance—we are not among those powers that pursue dollars for dependency. However, we draw the line at funding causes that harm our interests and our citizens.

Around the world, the United States seeks partners who are self-reliant, independent, and strong—nations that respect the interests of their people, the rights of their neighbors, and the principle of fairness and reciprocity in all agreements.

Under our new Africa Strategy, we will expand economic ties on the basis of mutual respect. We will help African nations take control of their own economic destinies and their own security needs. And, we will ensure that all U.S. foreign assistance in the region gets results for the American people.

I am honored to have had the opportunity to highlight the details of our plans here at Heritage today, and I look forward to taking your questions.

Thank you very much.

Still, No Gains

As noted in the previous chapter, Trump's New Africa Strategy has generated more criticisms than commendations. In the first instance, the idea of a national security adviser unveiling a diplomatic policy is, in itself, awkward. Common sense demands that a diplomatic function of such magnitude should be under the purview of the State Department, for it to be accorded the required attention. Adeola Akinremi, a policy expert from John Hopkins University, said it is part of a pattern to continuously demean the entire sub-Saharan region.

Predictably, many diplomatic experts have severally faulted the policy saying that whatever positive aspects of the strategy were lost as it requires African countries to choose between receiving US or Chinese development assistance, a situation, one of the experts, Tremann pointed out, is "harkening back to the cold war days when Africa's leaders had to strategically align themselves with the US or communist countries.

Clearly asking developing countries to choose between China and the US is a bad idea—perhaps most egregiously, in focusing so much on China, the new US African strategy implicitly treats African countries like a pawn in another great power rivalry", Tremann observed.

The last but by no means the least advantage that Africans stand to lose from Trump is that Trump, by his slur, has succeeded immensely in *reinforcing hurting stereotypes* about not only the region, but the people. Trump is reported as saying that Nigerians live in huts; tweets to "study closely", land seizures in South Africa and see the region as a *"shithole"*. Such profanities expose a stereotype that has good history of acceptability among majority of non-blacks.

Cara Anna, wrote in Associated Press that Trump rarely turns his attention to Africa…but when he does, it often backfires, mainly because of his vulgar remarks. Writing on "How Trump Degrades Us All," Masha Gessen, staff writer at *The New Yorker* stated, "Trump's *'shithole'* remark presented the media with a starker version of the daily Trumpian twitter conundrum…an ongoing degradation of the public sphere." Gessen added that, with black Africa, Trump is sure "giving voice to every stereotype he has ever heard.

CHAPTER EIGHT

The Stereotype Lives On

In one of the places I worked in New York, a colleague asked me if there were skyscrapers in Lagos, Nigeria. I initially wanted to take offence at the question, but on a second thought, I considered it a good opportunity to educate my colleague, a Caucasian, on the true state of things.

As a Nigerian American, who had lived for almost two decades in Lagos, Nigeria's largest city and central business district with about 17 million people, it was difficult where to start from in my response, but my mind quickly flashed to Manhattan in New York City. I then told my colleague, "I am sure you have never been to any part of Africa, but have you ever been to Manhattan in New York City?" She was surprised at my question, but hurriedly said, "Yes, of course." So, I told her, "If you have ever been to Manhattan, then conjure that same mental picture of Lagos."

To substantiate my point, I quickly pulled up, from Google images, pictures of not only Lagos, but also other big cities in Nigeria and black Africa for my colleague. Her countenance showed she felt I was offended by such a question. But I truly wasn't in any way offended because I thought she was asking to know, and I put in a great effort explaining to her what she did not know. Since that was not the first time of finding myself in a position to explain black Africa to someone, I actually took our interaction as an opportunity to correct the record.

A Common Challenge

My colleague at work happens to be just one of millions of people outside of sub-Saharan Africa or black Africa who know very little or nothing about the region, and the little they happen to know is unfortunately tainted by complete misinformation and stereotype.

My experience is by no means peculiar; it is just one of very many experiences faced by those that were born or grew up in black Africa, but now find themselves outside the region, especially in Europe and North America. Popular Nigerian author and feminist, Chimamanda Adiche, also recounted a similar experience in a TED talk. She recalled how, when she arrived at a university in the United

States, her roommate expressed astonishment at meeting someone from Africa who was not a victim of starvation - as if everyone in black Africa was starving.

But what is a stereotype? Without having to scour the encyclopedia, let us settle for a simple, straight forward meaning given by the *Glossary of Education Terms*, which defines stereotype as, "an oversimplified generalization about a group of people without regard for individual differences."

Stereotypes often cause people to make unfounded assumptions, mostly negative, about a people, place or thing.

This apt definition brings to fore, the predicament in which the places, peoples and cultures of the sub-Saharan African region have found themselves. This region, even with its over 1.1 billion of the world's population, continues to remain highly misunderstood, often snubbed, abandoned and utterly demeaned, like that from a sitting United States President, who is supposed to know better.

The region is often viewed through, according to Adichie, a single lens of unconscious bias, undue generalizations, mostly negative and with stereotype. From the weather, to the vegetation, animals, culture, idiosyncrasy of the people, health, psychology, security, socio-economic status in sub-Saharan

Africa, there are astounding misconceptions and stereotypes about them.

Maurice Oniango, a versatile, award-winning Kenyan journalist, writing on this issue on Africa.com listed ten common stereotypes about black Africa. Some of them include the belief that Africa is a country, even when there are 54 countries on the continent; that Africans speak *African*, even when there is no language known as *African* from the estimated 2000 or more languages spoken in the region. The list goes on, including the notion that, in black Africa, human beings and animals live together, akin to sometime in the mediaeval age; and that all Africans live in huts made of mud and dung, even when most cities on the continent boast of comparable skyscrapers and modern infrastructure anywhere in the world.

In this internet age, the stereotype is even made worse on social media. It is commonplace to read on sites like Twitter and Facebook messages like: *"I didn't know they had internet in Africa,"* or *"I didn't know Africans used computers,"* and a host of other derogatory comments.

This is apparently born out of the common misconception that has been advanced for decades that the continent lags in everything, including technological advancement. Some even add that in sub-Saharan Africa, there is no technological infrastructure, and that information technology is virtually non-existent. Indeed, some of the stereotypes go from being funny to being absurd.

What is not known, unfortunately, is that when it comes to technology, Africa has almost everything the rest of the world has. Although they may be slightly behind, technology is fast growing on the continent. For instance, Africa is said to be the fastest region when it comes to mobile growth. "It is estimated that over 67 per cent of the population on the continent have mobile phones, and 27 per cent have a device that can access the internet.

Africa is not only thriving on mobile technology and internet, but also other forms of technology that contributed immensely to the day-to-day life on the continent," Oniango wrote in Africa.com.

The Corruption Malaise

One area, though, where there is unanimity in the perception of black Africa is in the area of corruption. Over the years, sub-Saharan countries have been continuously ranked among the most corrupt nations by global corruption watchdog, Transparency International. In the 2016 corruption global corruption index, for instance, some African countries were very poorly ranked. Also, in the 2018 ranking, sub-Saharan countries dominate the top spots in the corruption index, with Equatorial Guinea, Guinea Bissau, Sudan, South Sudan and Somalia in that unholy group.

Without a doubt, corruption is endemic in black Africa, caused mostly by greed and ineptitude of the ruling class, emulated by the citizenry and enabled by colonial powers to stash away stolen money in developed economies and hold on to power, to the detriment of the country. For instance, several years after the death of General Sani Abacha, successive governments in Nigeria are still trying to ascertain the actual amount of money, which runs in billions of Nigerian naira, allegedly stolen by the late dictator and deposited in foreign banks. Consider major lead stories like the ones below:

"Following a series of negotiations between the Federal Government of Nigeria and the Government of Switzerland, the Swiss government will restitute $321 million of funds illicitly acquired by the family of the late Former President of Nigeria General Sani Abacha. In December 2014, a Swiss court ruled that the Swiss government should repatriate the funds on condition that the World Bank would monitor their use"—World Bank, Factsheet, December 4, 2017.

"The United States has taken control of more than $480 million looted by former Nigerian dictator Sani Abacha and his associates after a court

ruling, the Justice Department said on Thursday"---Reuters, August 7, 2014

"Abacha, accused of stealing over $4 billion during his five years in office, the World Bank will oversee dispersal of funds, including on social programs" ---CNN, December 6, 2017

As at early February 2020, *U.S News World Report*, quoting Reuters, reported that the United States and the British dependency of Jersey had agreed with Nigeria to repatriate more than $300 million in funds stolen by the former military ruler.

It is not as if corruption is peculiar to Africa, but the impunity with which those in the corridors of power misappropriate public funds and siphon them into private bank accounts is what is disconcerting.

Is Africa Truly Unsafe?

Another negatively impacting stereotype about black Africa is that the entire region is, a danger zone, a misconception that lead many to erroneously think that the continent is unsafe to visit. This has significantly deprived the region of income from tourism and Foreign Direct Investment (FDI).

Pictures of insecurity, riots, tensions and the sick, usually splashed all over the media, make people think nowhere is safe in the region. What is true, however, is that, as with any other place in the world, there are places with high crime rates that cannot be recommended for a visit, but there are also safe havens where crime rate is either negligible or almost nonexistent. It is worthy of note that every city in any country of the world has its fair share of rough neighborhoods, petty crime, or other safety-related problems, whether in Europe, North America, Australia or Asia.

Closely related to the above is yet another stereotype that Africa is disease-ridden. Long before the HIV/AIDS and Ebola outbreak, many people had speciously believed the region was filled with various diseases. Unfortunately, the outbreaks of such diseases as HIV and Ebola made matters even worse. What is not known, however, is that, as with most outbreaks, these diseases affect only some countries and not the entire region. For instance, the Ebola disease mostly affected a small number of countries: Sierra Leone, Liberia and Guinea.

It is worthy of note that the COVID-19 pandemic, which has become the deadliest infectious disease in recent times, did not emanate from Africa and black African countries have even, so far, recorded fewer casualties comparatively. Given that most African countries lack proper health care resources and personnel, but concerted efforts of multilateral institutions and nonprofits have had substantial positives impact in these countries.

Findings carried out by Aperian Global show that there are still other stereotypes about Africa, such as that it is always hot on the continent. The desert areas like Mali, Niger and Chad are hot but not all-year round. Conversely, there are also temperate landscapes in the region that have rainforest and snowy mountains. Examples are Jos in Nigeria, the Gembu area in Adamawa States of northeastern Nigeria and areas in South Africa. These areas experience below freezing point temperatures in some months during the year.

Promoters of Stereotypes

But the question remains, why the seemingly unending stereotypes about this part of the world and its peoples? The reasons are not far-fetched, with the greatest culprits being the media. The newsrooms' ideology of bad news being the good news makes virtually all western media, both locally and globally, embark on disaster reporting of the region. The international media relish crises, be they natural, environmental, social or political. They spotlight and highlight them for all to see.

A sensational disaster report of malnourished children in war-ravaged Somalia, for instance, gets banner headlines in print and screaming headlines in broadcast media and becomes the hot news story reported almost endlessly by the western media. This way, they feed the consciousness of the news consumers of that part of the world.

As a journalism student in Nigeria some decades ago, we studied disaster reporting, and it is regrettable to state that it is the mainstay of the media in developed economies. There is some positive aspect of disaster reporting, though - through spotlighting the disaster, help from far and near pours in.

Professor of journalism, City University of London, Suzanne Franks, wrote, "Always use the word 'Africa' or 'Darkness' or 'Safari' in your title. These are the opening words of a famous satirical essay by Kenyan writer Binyavanga Wainaina on how to write about Africa." According to Franks, international reporting of Africa focuses on the suffering of powerless victims, spiced with stunning shots of wildlife to achieve hopeless humanitarian crises or bizarre pictures. There is, she indicated, "a relentless negative image of suffering and impoverished victims, always experiencing famines, plagues and epidemics."

Analysis of news reports about black Africa shows that, on any given day, there are more negative than positive news stories, even when the situation portends positive. Take, for instance, when economies from the region were listed among the fastest growing economies in the mid-2000s, according to the World Bank. There arose a new media narrative that "Africa Rising" was not worth celebrating because it did not have a trickle-down effect.

Such commentators failed to also raise same thought process on tax cuts in some developed economies, which are ostensibly designed to favor the middle class but end up enriching the top one percent, without the envisaged trickledown effect. And this goes on in many spheres of human endeavor, where black Africa is stereotyped as never-do-well.

Besides the insidious role of the international media in misrepresenting sub-Saharan Africa, which has significantly succeeded in casting the entire region as no-good or good-for-nothings, even in the face of great feats recorded in all aspects of human endeavors, the complete ignorance on the part of the media consumers in the western world is also a pungent factor for the stereotype.

A peep into the curriculum of schools in the developed countries show very little or no mention of the outside world. From the elementary school to high school, children in the developed countries are seldom taught of anywhere else, except their own countries – the opposite of schools in Africa that teach even more about the outside world. Having travelled far and wide, I make bold to say that there is a lot to learn from in all parts of the world.

These children in the developed world therefore come out of school knowing very little or nothing outside their immediate environment and become so oblivious of the outside world - a good reason my well-educated colleague asked me if there were skyscrapers in Lagos.

Another reason for the unending stereotype is the fact that most people in the western world do not travel outside their countries of origin. If the saying that travelling is part of learning is anything to go by, then the inability of an individual to visit another part of the world and have firsthand knowledge of the environment, becomes an issue.

Inability to see and know what goes on elsewhere makes the individual, not only to believe the very negative reporting of those areas, but also help disseminate the flawed narrative.

There is yet another reason for the stereotypes. Some people do not just believe that anything good can come out of black Africa. Their perception is akin to the scriptural "Can anything good come out of Nazareth?" question asked by Nathanael in John 1:46.

To this set of people, the black African region, its peoples and places are the outer part of the earth, remote, out of the way; and the people are dumb, illiterate, poor, sick and probably living in huts and with animals; so they do not really matter.

This is the ultimate source of the inherent discrimination against blacks and people that are either from this part of the world or have the African heritage. It is also why anybody would say the place is made up of *"shithole"* countries. To this set of people, the stereotype sure lives on.

Without a doubt, it is an escalation of these stereotypes and the resultant demeaning and indignation of the black person that has propelled evolution of the Black Lives Matter (BLM) movement.

So far, this blacks advocacy movement is raising global consciousness on the worthiness of the black person.

Black Lives Matter should not be seen as solely an American internal affair, it is gaining global momentum, a rallying point for the stereotyped race. The recent worldwide protests after the the brutal killing of George Floyd is a testimony to this fact.

CHAPTER NINE

Are there Growth Potentials?

So, the question is, can anything good come out of black Africa to help change the perpetual negative perception of the place and its peoples?

It is an established fact that many people in this region are living far below their potentials, even though some economic development experts believe the region has a lot of potentials. These analysts say that, in virtually every sphere of human endeavors, the region and people of black Africa make their mark.

For instance, in debunking one of the stereotypes that black Africa is lacking in innovation, consultants at Aperian Global said the truth is that what people from these countries lack is access to qualitative education and not innovation. They quickly point at the following innovations, as examples recorded in recent times:

- Traffic-regulating robots. Thérèse Izay from Congo-Kinshasa invented humanlike robots to regulate traffic in Kinshasa. The robots function as a traffic light, combined with a crossing guard. In March 2015, there were five robots regulating traffic in this city, located in the Democratic Republic of the Congo.

- Drone in Nigeria. In December 2013, Nigeria's first unmanned aerial vehicle, commonly referred to as a drone, was created at the Nigerian Air Force School of Engineers. It can fly nonstop at 3,000 feet for nearly four hours. This is a significant accomplishment because it was Nigeria's first indigenous drone flight.

- Mercedes S-Class Interior Design. Steeve Burkhalter from Congo-Brazzaville designed the interior of the Mercedes' concept car.

Lion on the Move

In economic growth, Edward Miguel described the economic resurgence in the 2000s of many economies in the region as "Africa's Turn." According to Miguel, who devoted an entire book to this economic renaissance, Africa had always ranked lowest in the world in every economic and social indicator, but in the 1960s, it recorded intermittent recoveries, experienced another decline between

1976 to 1999, before experiencing phenomenal growth in the 2000s.

Researchers at Mckinsey Global Institute (MGI) stated that between 2000 and 2015, Gross Domestic Product (GDP) growth of Africa was at 5.4 per cent, a spike they described as "Lion on the move," fueled by Foreign Direct Investments (FDI) in the region.

According to MGI, since 2010, GDP growth has accelerated in around half of the largest 30 economies in Africa and decelerated in the other half. The decelerating economies include the continent's six largest—Nigeria, Egypt, South Africa, Algeria, Morocco, and Angola—while the accelerating countries are all in the sub-Saharan region: Botswana, Cameroon, Côte d'Ivoire, Democratic Republic of Congo, Ethiopia, Gabon, Ghana, Kenya, Madagascar, Namibia, Senegal, Tanzania, and Zimbabwe. To cap this spike in economic fortunes, in 2017, Nasdaq listed Ethiopia, Ghana and Cote d'Ivoire among the fastest growing economies in the world.

Growth and Stability Index

Like every other part of the globe, countries in the region are vulnerable to economic, social, and political shocks. Therefore, to better gauge stability at the country level, researchers at MGI developed an African Stability Index, which they hope can help businesses and investors understand their portfolio risk and also help policy makers understand and address their own countries' vulnerabilities.

The index highlights the diverging growth and stability trends that economies in the region have been experiencing since MGI published its first report on Africa's economies in 2010. Three distinct groups emerge from the MGI index as:

- **Stable growers.** These countries, which accounted for 19 percent of Africa's GDP in 2015, posted an average GDP growth of 5.8 percent a year between 2010 and 2015— higher than the 2.9 percent a year global average over this period—and demonstrated relatively high levels of stability. sub-Saharan countries in this group includes Botswana, Côte d'Ivoire, Ethiopia, Kenya, Mauritius, Rwanda, Senegal, Tanzania, and Uganda. These countries, typically not dependent on resources for growth, are smaller economies that are progressing with economic reform and increasing their competitiveness.

- **Vulnerable growers.** These countries, which accounted for 35 percent of African GDP in 2015, achieved average GDP growth of 5.1 percent a year over the past five years but had relatively low levels of stability. This group includes countries

161

heavily dependent on resources, such as Nigeria, Angola, and Zambia, as well as countries such as the Democratic Republic of Congo, which have clear potential but need to improve their security, governance, or macroeconomic stability.

- **Slow growers.** These countries, which accounted for 46 percent of Africa's GDP in 2015, together grew at 1.3 percent per year between 2010 and 2015—less than the 2.9 percent a year global average over that period—and have had varying degrees of stability. This group includes the countries affected by the Arab Spring—Libya, Egypt, and Tunisia. It also includes South Africa, which is experiencing slow growth and high unemployment in spite of promising opportunities that could spur development.

Generally, analysts at MGI gave a strong ray of hope indicating that "despite African economies diverging in their growth paths from 2010 to 2015, the continent's overall outlook remains promising. Africa's collective GDP is still expanding faster than the world average, and it is forecast to accelerate over the next five years to become the world's second-fastest-growing region once again."

In the longer term, they listed four factors that could have a transformative effect on the continent's economies and their pace of growth, namely: (i)

Africa is the world's fastest urbanizing region; (ii) the region has a young population and growing workforce that would be larger than those of either China or India by 2034; (iii) there is huge potential from accelerating technological change; and (iv) there is an abundance of mineral resources.

Natural Resources

In no other area are the potentials in sub-Saharan more visible and attractive than in natural resources, especially mineral reserves. The region is said to be so endowed with mineral deposits that it led to the much talked about scramble for Africa of the late 1960s and early 1970s. This was a period when virtually all the developed economies were scrambling to have a shot at the abundant mineral wealth of the region.

Reports say, in 2011 for instance, the region exported 6.5 percent of the world's total mineral exports, a greater potential that is largely underexplored. Let's look at a few summaries as given by researchers at Aperian Global.

- **Industrial diamond** - Africa accounts for about 46 percent of the world's diamonds. Botswana, Tanzania, Democratic Republic of Congo and Sierra Leone are the top exporters.

- **Bauxite** - Earns Guinea a great deal of foreign exchange, and the country exports about 8 percent of the world's total.

- **Platinum Group Metals** - Africa exports most of the world's platinum group metals, contributing an astounding 75 percent of the world's total output. South Africa contributes most of this metal.

- **Phosphate rock** - Senegal and South Africa account for most of the continent's phosphate rock exports.

- **Gold** - As the most mined resource in Africa, it is responsible for about 21 percent of the world's total. Countries exporting gold include South Africa, Ghana and Tanzania, among many others.

- **Vermiculite** - South Africa and Zimbabwe export most of the continent's vermiculite.

- **Cobalt** - Zambia provides the world with a great deal of cobalt, and the country is highly dependent on this export.

- **Zirconium** - Much of the world's supply of zirconium is mined in and exported from South Africa.

Black Africa's rich mineral wealth is corroborated by the MGI research which stated that "Africa contains 60 percent of the world's unutilized but potentially available cropland, as well as the world's largest reserves of vanadium, diamonds, manganese, phosphate, platinum-group metals, cobalt, aluminum, chromium, and gold. It is responsible for 10 percent of global exports of oil and gas, 9 percent of copper, and 5 percent of iron ore."

With a maximum crude oil production capacity of 2.5 million barrels per day, Nigeria for instance, has perennially ranked as Africa's largest producer of oil and the sixth largest oil producing country in the world. The country is said to even have a greater potential for gas than oil. According to the World Energy Council, "Nigeria's role as a major natural gas player is due to its large base of proved natural gas reserves and importance as a natural gas exporter. As of 2014, Nigeria had 5,111 bcm of proved natural gas reserves. This makes the country the ninth most proved natural gas reserves in the world and the most proved reserves in Africa."

Also, from the region is Angola, whose oil output, as at October 2018, rose to 1.533 million barrels per day, according to the Organization of Petroleum Exporting Countries (OPEC).

It is in recognition of Africa's enormous potentials

in virtually all spheres - arts, agriculture, commerce, technology, sports, religion, culture - that John Sullivan, deputy secretary of state in Angola, stated that the Trump administration plans to make expansion of trade and investment a key priority. If and when that will happen is a matter of conjecture.

So, one can confidently say that black Africa is not made up of "*shithole*" countries, with everybody living in muds and huts, naked, hungry and perhaps with animals according to the stereotypes. They sure have the potentials for tomorrow. As aptly described by the US Deputy Secretary of States, Africa is indeed, "the dynamic continent of the future."

About the Author

Williams Ekanem is a Nigerian-American journalist and communications specialist. He worked for many years as a Business/Financial Editor in Nigeria, contributor to African Business magazine published in London, and reported from the White House, the US Congress and the World Bank in Washington D.C. He is an editorial contributor to many media organizations.

As a communications specialist, Williams has developed marketing communications strategies for startups, nonprofits and individuals.

A teacher of the word of God and leader in ministry, Williams' passion in inspiring people to take a leap of faith and actualize their potentials informed the writing of his first book, *Faith: The Believers' Rod*.